Finding Time
for Fathering

Dear Howard,
thanks for being
part of the
Fathers' Forum.
Best wishes,
Bruce

FINDING TIME FOR FATHERING

Mitch Golant, Ph.D.
with Susan Golant

FAWCETT COLUMBINE · NEW YORK

A Fawcett Columbine Book
Published by Ballantine Books
Copyright © 1992 by Mitch Golant and Susan Golant

All rights reserved under International and Pan-American Copyright Conventions. Published in the United States by Ballantine Books, a division of Random House, Inc., New York, and simultaneously in Canada by Random House of Canada Limited, Toronto.

Library of Congress Catalog Card Number: 91-90630

ISBN: 0-449-90558-6

Cover photograph: Tony Stone Worldwide

MANUFACTURED IN THE UNITED STATES OF AMERICA
First Edition: June 1992

10 9 8 7 6 5 4 3 2 1

For
My father, Sam
My father-in-law, Arthur
And my mother's father, William Stock, whom I never
knew but whose soul lives on in blessed memory

Acknowledgments

This book is an outgrowth of more than a decade of encouragement and support. First, I would like to thank Dr. Norma Radin of the University of Michigan, who opened her files and ideas to me and encouraged me to develop a community-based program for fathers. I'm also grateful to Dr. Adele Sheele, who many years ago helped me map a strategy that has culminated with the publication of this book. Bob Tabian, our agent at International Creative Management, believed and supported us in the project. Virginia Faber at Balantine Books tirelessly edited the manuscript and with perspicacious questions ultimately helped us find the book within the book.

My thinking about fathers has been deeply influenced by pioneers in the men's movement and fathering: Michael Lamb, Ph.D.; Warren Farrell, Ph.D.; Robert Bly; Ronald Levant, Ph.D.; Samuel Osherson, Ph.D.; Martin Greenberg, M.D.; Robert S. Weiss, Ph.D.; and Arlie Hochschild, Ph.D. I'm also indebted to the original group of men and women who organized and mounted the Los Angeles Fatherhood Forum. In that regard, I would especially like to thank Rick Porter, whose selfless devotion to this project (and to young children) has been a source of strength.

My friends Alan Gross, Sheila Gross, Jan Smith, Al Rabinowitz, Dick Campbell, Luba Fischer, Rich Koren, Audrey Koren, Jock Hearn, Jonathan Omer-man, Daniel Polish, Bette Harrell, Jan Harrell, Al Robbins, Bruce Phillips, Rick Friedberg, Harold Benjamin, and, especially, Michael Braun have shared intimately their concerns as fathers and mothers, men and women. I'm also indebted to all the men who participated in my Fathering Workshops. They shared their lives and thereby changed mine.

I would like to thank my family. My children Cherie and Aimee have helped me to become the father that they instinctively knew I could be. My father and mother, Sam and Evelyn Golant, and my in-laws, Arthur and Mary Kleinhander and Henriette Kleinhander, have been cheerleaders in this project.

Finally, my wife, Susan, who first saw the Tom Sawyer in me and thought that others could benefit and have some fun. More important, as the co-author she not only has helped convey my voice throughout this book, but also has challenged me through unrelenting questions to hone and essentialize my thinking. And ultimately, we are two souls who, out of infinite possibility, have cherished each other, and thus through love have often merged into one.

Contents

Contents

Contents

PART 1

Your Changing Role as Father

1

Waxing the Chevy and Other Beginnings

ONE sunny afternoon in 1978 I was in the driveway waxing my new Chevy, a favorite Sunday pastime. My younger daughter, Aimee (about four years old at the time), rumbled up on her Big Wheels.

"Can I help?" she asked, eyes bright with excitement.

"Well . . ." The truth was, I took pride in my hobby and didn't want to deal with clumsy fingers and smudgy chrome. "Well . . ." This was my form of relaxation and I guarded it jealously. Yet my daughter was fervently asking for attention and I was in a position to give it. "Tell you what," I offered in a moment of inspiration. "Here's a sponge. Why don't you fill the old brown bucket with clean water and you can wash your Big Wheels right here next to my car."

"Great idea, Dad," she said, and she was off to do as I had suggested.

Before long, Aimee's best friend, Melissa, rode up and took a turn with the sponge on her tricycle. Then Cherie, our older daughter, and her friend Sara came by on their two-wheelers. In fact, within fifteen minutes, half a dozen neighborhood kids and I were assembled on the lawn busily engaged in car polishing, bike washing, talking, singing, and joking.

My wife, Sue, looked out the front window and had to laugh. "You know," she told me later, "you looked just like Tom Sawyer out there. You had those kids eating out of your hand. I'll bet you could teach some of your skills to other men. There sure is a need for it."

She had a good point. As a clinical psychologist, I had noted that many men had a hard time including their children in their lives in a meaningful way. Conversely, men didn't know how to involve themselves in their children's lives. Though they would rarely admit it, their children's world seemed a woman's domain, and so they often felt excluded from a close relationship with their kids.

Intrigued by my wife's idea, I spent several years delving into research on fathering and men's issues. I was surprised by my findings:

• I could locate no famous paintings or sculpture that depicted men nurturing or even holding children.
• Most classical psychoanalytic literature emphasizes the mother's impact on a child's development. Yet developmental psychologists had found that a man also has a profound, albeit different, effect on the child's development.
• Men don't play with children in the same way their wives do. They have a unique form of interaction that is special in its own right.
• Indeed, men have a deep hunger to create meaningful relationships with their children despite insecurities and a perceived lack of ability.

I next created the Finding Time for Fathering program in Los Angeles. The program consists of a free workshop and a four-session course in which I teach men how to become more active in parenting. The people who come to my classes fall into several groups:

• Men who feel harried and hassled by their professional lives and who want to spend more time with their kids.
• Men in conflict with their wives over parenting styles and child care duties who are looking for a way to reduce the tension in their homes.
• Men about to have their first baby who don't want to repeat their own father's model, yet don't know how to begin making changes.
• Men who are about to have a second child and feel at a loss as to how to juggle the increase in family and financial demands.
• Men who are about to begin a second family and want to do it "right" this time. They don't want to miss out again.
• Divorced men and women who have custody of their children. The women, in particular, are looking to make up for the father's absence.

Participants learn about the unique role that fathers play and share their concerns within a supportive environment. They are often amazingly frank about their family struggles despite an audience of relative strangers.

The group composition changes from month to month, offering a kaleidoscope of male points of view over the ten years of this program's existence. Hundreds of men, from car assemblers and electric power linemen to business executives, engineers, and ophthalmologists, have attended, and many of their concerns and comments appear throughout this book.

During this time, I also helped found and stage the Los Angeles Fatherhood Forum, a weekend event that brought hundreds of men together to deal with their concerns and their roles as father. This book is an outgrowth of these experiences, coupled with my practice as a licensed clinical psychologist and a leader of "Daddy and Me" classes. And, of course, my daughters (now in college) provided some of the best training of all.

Today, the world of fatherhood and the vast impact that fathers can have on their children is just coming to the attention of millions of men around the country. This is great news. The more men are involved in the raising of their children, the better for all concerned.

Why It's Important to Find the Time

Both children and fathers benefit hugely from time spent together. Although most psychoanalytic research investigates a mother's impact, new research by child developmentalists has shown that fathers have profound influence on their youngsters' social adjustment, intellectual growth, and sex role development (see Chapter 5). Moreover, the more time dads spend with their youngsters, the better they are at correctly identifying their kids' developmental progress, and the more appropriate their interactions are. Participating in youngsters' lives can be great fun and will help enhance family intimacy.

On the other hand, anthropologists and sociobiologists have found that a father's emotional distance can have profound negative repercussions. Dr. Louise B. Silverstein of New York University explained in an article in the October 1991 issue of *American Psychologist* that "research clearly documents the direct correlation between father absence and higher rates of aggressive behavior in sons, sexually precocious behavior in daughters, and more rigid sex stereotypes in children of both sexes." This may even be true in divorces. Citing recent research, Silverstein maintained that sons raised by divorced mothers exhibit more dysfunctional behavior than sons raised in intact families. Clearly, it's important to be emotionally and physically available to children.

Besides, fathering is not a one-way relationship; it provides benefits for the father, too. Studies have shown that the more time a father spends with his kids, the closer and warmer—the more mutually enriching—their relationship becomes. For instance, Dr. Graeme Russell of Macquarie University in Australia investigated families in which fathers either shared or took the majority of responsibility for child care. Sixty-nine percent of the men in this study reported better rapport with their children and felt positive about the relationships. Other studies confirm that fathers who spend time with their children really enjoy the experience.

Increased sensitivity is one of the more tangible rewards of involved fathering. In fact, in Russell's study the fathers reported that it was not just the increased time that made the difference for them. The men felt they really learned to understand their children when they took sole responsibility for them, and as a result they felt more confident and effective as parents. Mastering a new, more nurturing role boosted their self-esteem.

Ideally, your involvement with your kids can take the form of a regular period, whether ten minutes a day, an hour a week, or a day every month. Your child may have your complete attention, or, as I'll show you in Chapters 9 and 10, you can incorporate fathering activities into otherwise mundane routines like driving, preparing dinner, or washing the car. If you honor this commitment and can be flexible and responsive, lifelong closeness, intimacy, and emotional health will result. Specific strategies and activities are given in Parts 2 and 3.

The Father's Dilemma

Let's face it. Although you may understand the benefits of family involvement, if you're a man, the expectation still exists that you be the breadwinner. Despite monumental shifts in our society during the last two decades and the entrance of many more women into the work force (see Chapter 2), most men still perceive themselves as the principal (if not sole) financial providers for their families.

You may like your work. Like many men, you may derive satisfaction from your ability to make money and to achieve professional success. On the other hand, you may struggle with your own expectations and feel the emotional burden of being the breadwinner.

If you're like a growing number of men today, you may feel drawn into a conflict between your desire to participate in your children's world and your wish to realize the real needs that work fulfills for you. This emotional tug-of-war can create feelings of guilt, anger, and resentment.

I, too, have felt overwhelmed by the competing demands of family and career. I have experienced the wide range of roles available to men in the late twentieth century. I have shared and relinquished responsibility for child care; I have worked part time, full time, overtime, and double time; I have been the sole breadwinner and, conversely, have known the joys of being a househusband.

I became a father at 6:33 P.M. on February 13, 1970, at the tender age of twenty-three. My wife, Susan, was twenty-one; we had not yet been married a full year. I had just taken my very first "real" job as a teacher, and we were both still in graduate school.

Cherie came into the world with a full head of black hair and the cutest smile imaginable. She was born by cesarean section, and in those days (they now seem antediluvian) fathers were not allowed in the delivery room. In fact, when Sue had inquired of her obstetrician about natural child-birth and breastfeeding, which were just coming back into vogue, her physician simply turned up his nose. "Whatever would you want to do *that* for?" was his reaction. We were too young and too intimidated to even think about challenging him.

I remember those early years of Cherie's life as a time of innocence. To be sure, they were hectic and stressful. Not only were we adjusting to our new marriage, new apartment, new job, and new baby, but we were also struggling financially. Nevertheless, our home was filled with love for each other and for our Cherie. We were determined to make the best of it.

My job as a teacher afforded me a certain degree of stability and the benefit of finishing my workday at 3 P.M.

We alternated evenings taking classes in graduate school. The nights Sue was at college, I prepared dinner, fed Cherie, played with her, bathed her, and put her to bed. We spent the weekends taking turns studying and babysitting. I found that I had lots of time, if not with Sue, at least alone with my daughter. And I was off during the summers, when we all spent long, lazy days at the beach.

I had great fun with Cherie. Even as a baby she had a wonderful sense of humor, and I loved nothing more than to "giggle her up." We played silly games together. I put on funny hats, built block cities that she relished destroying, made up stories using themes from my own life, let her climb all over me, and engaged in our version of hide-and-seek that we called the Blankie Game. I even taught her about letters and reading. (After all, I was a remedial reading teacher.)

By 1972 I had finished my master's degree in counseling and guidance and found a new job as a child welfare and attendance counselor. The work challenged and interested me. In fact, since I had come this far, I decided to go for a doctorate in counseling from the University of Southern California.

A year later Sue finished her degree in French literature and shortly thereafter gave birth to our second daughter, Aimee. My wife was pretty exhausted and decided that rather than pursuing her plans for a Ph.D. in French, she would stay home and be a "mommy" for a while. Caught in the cross fire of the exploding women's movement, she yearned for some time to reevaluate what she wanted to do with her life.

This suited all of us. I needed additional support now that I was working on my doctorate, and the children were still quite young. Yet I began to feel the increased pressure of being responsible for three other human beings. With the birth of Aimee, we longed for more room, a yard, a dog, a neighborhood. Sue began looking for a house in earnest. Many an evening I didn't make it home for dinner. I just went straight to class from work. I would awaken at 4 A.M., when the house was quiet and I was sure to be undisturbed, in order to keep up with the course load. It became apparent that unlike many of our friends and peers who had delayed marriage and children, who had neatly organized their lives into a series of well-planned events, we were attempting to do everything—marriage, children, house, education, career—all at once. It was exhausting.

The situation reached an almost intolerable pitch in 1975, when the university required me to establish residency. That meant taking at least three courses each semester for one school year. The class hours were difficult enough to manage, but in truth, with our new mortgage payments and Cherie's nursery school, we just couldn't afford the tuition. So I became a graduate teaching assistant, which meant that I spent every night of the week at the university, either learning or teaching.

Of course, this didn't sit very well with my family. Sue, who had gone back to teaching French part time at private schools, felt abandoned. She complained—and rightfully so—that she was no different from a single mother. I was just not around, and when I was home, I was either studying or sleeping. On my part, I felt that I had to work those crazy hours in order to provide for our future. Despite our best intentions, we had fallen into the traditional family setup and nearly wound up getting divorced. All in all, it took me seven years to finish my doctorate. In fact, I remember bursting out of my study in the middle of Aimee's sixth birthday party with the exciting news that I had finished writing my dissertation.

In the meantime, my responsibilities at work had increased tremendously. I was promoted to the post of assistant principal in charge of guidance at an intermediate school of 1,500 preadolescents, many of whom were involved in gangs. The stress of my schooling, the job, and the forty-minute drive home in bumper-to-bumper Los Angeles freeway traffic began to take its toll. Now it was my turn to feel exhausted and to want the time to reevaluate the direction of my life. As a trainee for the clinical psychologist license, I was required to amass 3,000 hours of supervised clinical work in order to qualify for the California licensing exam. I didn't see how I could work those many hours with patients and continue in my job. So, with my wife's encouragement, I left the school district. To finance the move, we sold a piece of property, withdrew my funds from the state retirement plan, and lived on our capital for the year. Sue increased the hours that she taught. And I was suddenly a househusband.

It was pretty tough going from a salary of $3,000 a month to $300 with no benefits. But perhaps more unnerving were the snide remarks. While I was out walking the dog or watering the lawn, male neighbors on their way to or from work would wave somewhat ruefully, making comments like, "What's for dinner?" and "Where's your apron?"

In truth, I rather enjoyed my year at home as I worked on building my practice and collecting hours. In fact, it was during this period that I created the Finding Time for Fathering program. In addition, I became the neighborhood "daddy." If a child on the block got hurt, if someone was in trouble, friends called on me to help out. I cooked the family dinner twice a week, shopped for groceries, and helped around the house. I felt a certain pride in my expanding repertoire. What a welcome relief from the years of long work hours I had come to endure. And, as an extra benefit, I was able to spend more time with my children.

As my psychology practice grew over the next five years, I became a full-time worker once more. Again, I found myself challenged to balance my time away from home with my time as a dad. To be sure, my kids had grown and didn't require the kind of constant care that they had as toddlers. But adolescents, too, need and want attention and guidance. Even now, with two daughters away at college, I am still called upon to provide loving encouragement, set occasional limits, lend a sympathetic ear—and pay for tuition.

This book and the program I'll be advocating are the outgrowth of these professional and personal experiences. As a party to the social and cultural changes that have occurred over the past twenty years, I have found that there are straightforward solutions to the dilemmas fathers face. When given the proper tools, men can and do learn how to participate effectively in their children's growth and development. I'll be sharing the mechanics with you throughout these chapters.

How to Find the Time

In *Raising Your Child to Be a Mensch,* **Rabbi Neil Kurshan** ruefully reflects on the three types of so-called quality time he spends with his three children. The first he calls "Split-Brain Time." That's when only one side of his brain is involved with his kids; the other side is still busily engaged in work-related thoughts. The second he calls "Timed Time." This, he says, "is best characterized by declarations such as, 'Okay, you children have ten minutes to get in bed and fall asleep.' " He goes on to say, "On a really bad day, I settle for the 'Quality Greeting'—a brief 'Hi there!' or 'Sleep tight'—usually uttered from a comfortable chair, just before I drift off to sleep." I am sure that we can all recognize ourselves in Rabbi Kurshan's description. He suggests that we reorient our priorities—taking a day off from work once in a while or changing to a less demanding job—so that we can spend more time with our children.

Although Rabbi Kurshan's thought is noble and his heart is in the right place, I'm afraid that he is being somewhat naive. Perhaps temporarily—a week, a month, a year—we may cut back on our work hours, but usually it's not that easy. To tell a man to just work less is like telling an alcoholic to just stop drinking. Rather, it's necessary to rethink the whole concept of available time in a realistic way. Changing your perception of time takes encouragement, thought, and reeducation.

Finding Time for Fathering is meant to support you in whatever you need to do to provide for your family's physical, financial, and emotional well-being. This book is not going to make you feel guilty because you have to work.

Instead, it's going to help you feel good about your role as a father.

Well, you might ask, if there are only twenty-four hours in the day and I'm at my limit already, how is it possible to find more time? Good question. Of course, you can't add hours to the day—nor would you want to. What to do? Do you remember the architect Miës van der Rohe's dictum, "Less is more"? Since you can't create more time, it's up to you to use what little time you do have more efficiently. The Finding Time for Fathering program helps make the most of what you've got by changing attitudes as well as behaviors. Before altering your actions, you must first reorient your thinking.

The Finding Time for Fathering program consists of the following:

• Understanding the double bind of modern fatherhood (see Chapter 2).
• Recognizing your capacity to nurture (see Chapter 3).
• Identifying how your father influenced your view of involvement (see Chapter 4).
• Valuing the profound social, emotional, and intellectual impact you have on your children (see Chapter 5).
• Learning about authoritative fathering—the most effective approach to interactions (see Chapters 5 and 6).
• Setting limits with love so you don't fall into an authoritarian role or waste most of your available time arguing over your children's misbehavior (see Chapters 5 and 6).

• Appreciating child development in order to match
your expectations and interactions to your children's
abilities and interests (see Chapters 7 and 8).
• Using bits of time more enjoyably by regarding routine
encounters with your children as opportunities for
enhancing affection and closeness (see Chapters 9 and
10).
• Playing, especially in intimacy-enhancing
noncompetitive games (see Chapter 10).
• Engaging your youngsters in your work and hobbies
(see Chapters 10 and 11).
• Maintaining your fathering connection even if you
must be separated from your family (see Chapter 12).

Finding Time for Fathering is a shift in attitude from "How
can I get to the bank and cleaners and carwash with my kid
in tow," to "How can I make these excursions and errands
more enjoyable so we can get closer, and learn about each
other's worlds."

How to Use This Book

Part 1 of *Finding Time for Fathering* establishes the context
of social and personal pressure that fathers feel. Our society has come a long way from the idea of the traditional,
authoritarian father. Sometimes the changes have occurred at a dizzying pace, causing confusion in our relationships with our spouses and children and within
ourselves. We'll take an in-depth look at the "new" father's
dilemmas and dispel the myth that fathers are nonnurtur-
ing members of the family. We'll also consider the impact

of your own father on you and how it affects your parenting style. You'll learn how to make changes, where necessary.

Part 2 presents an organizing framework for your new fathering activities. It explores the latest research on fathers' impact on children's social, intellectual, and sex role development. Indeed, the better you understand your vital importance, the more likely you'll be motivated to find the time to spend with your kids. You'll learn how and why the authoritative fathering style (lots of warmth coupled with appropriate expectations) produces the most successful and happiest children and how to apply its principles, especially when disciplining. Properly dispensed discipline is important not only for your children's growth and development but also for your own feelings about your role as father.

In addition, Part 2 explores child development from pregnancy to adolescence from a father's point of view. The information will help you tailor expectations and activities to your children's developmental stages, thereby lessening frustration for everyone. This section also tackles the sensitive issue of your impact on sexual development, which can affect your youngsters' ability to create intimate relationships in the future.

Part 3 provides specific suggestions for everyday activities, applying principles you've mastered earlier. You'll learn about the paradox of "quality" time and how to enrich the moments you actually spend with your family. Part 3 also covers a loving approach to competitive and noncompetitive play. It presents a variety of open-ended, imaginative games to let your kids into your world and, conversely, to let you see how *they* think. It also shows you how to incorporate your children into your daily work with very little effort and a lot of fun and how to maintain your connection if you must be separated from them.

Since the concepts build upon one another, it's best to read *Finding Time for Fathering* straight through. If you're harried and hurried, you may go to the parts you find most meaningful. But do try to backtrack when you have more time, since it's important to understand the theories underlying the practice. If you find even one suggestion useful in helping you relate to your children, then I'll have accomplished my goal in writing this book.

Think of It as an Investment

Most likely you will have several jobs or careers during your lifetime. Yet fathering is perhaps the only "career" that endures. It is an essential part of your life as a man. It's important, then, for you to consider your family goals as carefully as you do your career goals. After all, if you make, save, and spend time for fathering, you are investing in your relationships and can only reap the dividends of an enriched and loving family as your children grow older.

The importance of finding time was brought home to me several years ago, immediately after the massive earthquake in the San Francisco Bay area. At the time, our daughter Cherie was a student at the University of California at Santa Cruz. Literally, she was sitting on top of the epicenter of the second-worst quake in this country's history. Unable to make a connection by phone, we helplessly and anxiously watched the devastation on TV, praying that our daughter had been spared.

At 9:30 P.M., when Cherie's call finally got through, I

paused and reflected on how precious our lives are and how fragile. It was then that I realized *Finding Time for Fathering* had taken on a new urgency. Finding time exists only because we are alive and can express the love we feel. Finding time exists when we can enjoy the moment, for none of us knows what lies ahead. Finally, finding time is crucial because life is short and infinitely precious.

2

The Dilemma of the "New" Father

I ENVISIONED this chapter as a sort of "cheerleading" section. Times have changed and fathers are becoming more involved. Let's go for it! Rah! Rah! Rah!

Certainly, the numbers and the earnestness of the men coming to my office point in that direction. Evidence also abounds in the press. A March 1989 article in *Newsweek*, for example, highlights just how quickly our feelings (although not necessarily our behavior) regarding work and family have shifted. A survey of 100,000 employees of Du Pont showed that the number of men interested in the option of part-time work nearly doubled from 18 percent in 1985 to 33 percent in 1988. "Companies have been slow to recognize that some men want a career-and-family track of their own," the author of the article noted.

A *New York Times* report on this same survey elaborates. Faith Wohl, director of Du Pont's Work Force Partnering Division, was quoted as saying, "We have found dramatic evidence that the men's attitudes toward work-family questions is very quickly coming to resemble women's." The report went on to explain that "in just those three years, . . . male employees had become significantly more troubled by problems like relocation, finding child care at the last minute and synchronizing their vacations with school vacations. In some categories, the men were just as concerned about such things as the women." Indeed, an unrelated 1990 poll of men between the ages of eighteen and twenty-four conducted by *Time* magazine found that "an astonishing 48 percent expressed an interest in staying home with their children."

These attitudinal changes have occurred with dizzying rapidity. When have so many men described themselves as willing to give up full-time work to create time for their families? At first glance, it seemed to me that our full and equitable involvement with our kids was just around the corner. The image of the "new" father—nurturing, involved, ready to pitch in at a moment's notice, or even willing and able to take full responsibility for parenting— seemed to emerge logically from our outmoded sex role stereotypes.

However, fathers today still face some painfully tough dilemmas. Even though we want to become more involved, powerful forces within ourselves and our culture keep us from doing so. Colin McEnroe, a columnist for the Hartford, Connecticut, *Courant* who had taken some six weeks off from his job ostensibly to start a new book but in fact to get better acquainted with his one-year-old, captures the feeling best in an essay published in the October 27, 1990, issue of the *San Jose Mercury News:*

It turns out that I like diapering and bottle-feeding and cooking and dog-tending and lying on a blanket with my little boy, gazing up at the intersections of sky and tree. So does my wife. In fact, we like doing all that stuff together, and neither of us is all that crazy about having a job.

So here is what I figure:

We need a husband.

This extra husband would, of course, keep out of the way as much as possible (especially in the bedroom) and would work overtime to pay for the family's many expenses.

Legal and matrimonial issues aside, why does McEnroe's proposal evoke a smile of recognition in us? In this fantasy ménage à trois, McEnroe's having his cake and eating it too. Certainly, we can all identify with his longings to spend all of his time with his son while the family coffers magically remain full. McEnroe touches a deeper issue as well. Our new attitudes about family involvement generally do not match our behavior. Even though we may be interested in or express our desire to be included in our children's lives to a greater extent, many of us have not found a way to act in accordance with our new beliefs. *Harper's* September 1991 index showed, for example, that while 31 percent of the Fortune 1000 companies offer paternity leave, only 1 percent of eligible men actually take advantage of it.

In fact, the 1990 Virginia Slims Opinion Poll conducted by Roper found that 53 percent of women surveyed thought that "most men are interested in their work and life outside the home and don't pay much attention to things going on at home." This was up from 39 percent of the women surveyed in 1970. While only an opinion poll, this is a sobering commentary, indeed.

What keeps us from being more involved? The reasons for the disparity between our desires and our actions are complex and are probably rooted in centuries-old culturally ingrained patterns of relating to our work and our families.

In truth, fathers today (in contrast to our own fathers, whose roles were more clearly defined) are caught in a labyrinth of contradictory expectations, double messages, and triple binds. Here are some components of the "new" father's dilemma:

• We are driven to create meaningful relationships with our children, yet we feel guilty because of the enormous energy we devote to work outside the home—work from which we still derive great satisfaction.

• We feel compelled to become more involved in parenting (or our wives demand that we do so), yet we feel unconscious pressure (from our buddies, bosses, and surprisingly our wives) to behave exactly as our fathers did and leave the bulk of the parenting to women.

• We perceive our working for the family as an expression of our love, nurturance, and support, yet that very work takes us away from our loved ones and causes discord.

• We are torn between our role as the principal provider of the family and the image of the idealized nurturing man.

As Dr. Graeme Russell of Macquarie University and Dr. Norma Radin of the University of Michigan explained in a 1983 article on paternal participation in child rearing, our increased involvement gives rise to closer and better relationships with our children and spouses, a feeling of greater satisfaction with our parenting role, and increased self-esteem. But these benefits must be measured against the intensified conflicts we feel at work and with our spouses, children, and male friends; the tension between demands of home and work; and the loss of career advancement.

There are no easy answers. Setting aside fifteen minutes a day to read a story or play ball with a child does not solve the problem. The first step is for us to become aware of the cultural tug-of-war that keeps our family-work commitments frozen in traditional patterns while it compels us to act differently.

Two recently published books—one from the woman's point of view, the other from the man's—elaborate on the predicaments that men, women, and their children face today. Both books agree on one issue: There still exists an overriding cultural bias dictating that men are responsible for the family through their work, while women are responsible for the family through the care of children.

The Social Context from a Woman's Perspective

According to the U.S. Bureau of Labor Statistics, in March 1990 about 54 percent of married women with children age one and under were employed outside the home. That's more than double the rate of 24 percent in 1970. Indeed, according to the government tally, today nearly 74 percent of all married women with school-age children are employed. This fundamental change in our society has placed an additional burden on mothers as well as fathers.

Dr. Arlie Hochschild, a University of California at Berkeley sociology professor, is the author of *The Second Shift: Working Parents and the Revolution at Home.* She observed and interviewed "typical" dual-career couples raising children under the age of six over an eight-year period (from 1980 to 1988), spending many hours in these families' homes, taking notes as the couples cooked dinner, shopped, watched TV, visited with friends, played with and bathed their children, and argued over who should take responsibility for child care, housework, and wage earning.

Hochschild discovered that women with full-time employment outside the home work an average of fifteen hours longer each week than do their spouses. Most returned from their day jobs only to deal with an evening of meal preparation, laundry, household chores, and child care "maintenance" duties, such as feeding and bathing. That time added up to *"an extra month of twenty-four-hour days a year.* Over a dozen years it was an extra year of twenty-four-hour days." Hochschild labeled this the "second shift."

Although many couples believe in equity, few actually implement it. According to Hochschild's study, only about 20 percent of the men surveyed shared in the household and family chores. This 20 percent felt just as pressured as their wives to balance their careers with the demands of young children.

The other 80 percent of the men in the study, however, still experienced some pressure from their wives to become more involved. They were, Hochschild noted, "often indirectly just as deeply affected as their wives by the need to do that work, through the resentment their wives feel toward them, and through their need to steel themselves against that resentment."

Hochschild ascribed this disparity in household involvement to a broader social tension between "faster-changing women and slower-changing men." Today's women differ more from their mothers than men do from their fathers. In particular, since 1960 many more women have moved out into the work force, and with much greater speed than men have shown in becoming involved within the home. Nevertheless, according to Hochschild, "even when husbands happily shared the hours of work, their wives felt more responsible for home and children."

On the positive side, those few men who were more involved with their children had a much richer view of what it meant to be a father. Hochschild found that these men discussed their fathering in much the same way that their wives talked about mothering. The uninvolved fathers, on the other hand, believed that their role consisted simply of disciplining their children and teaching them sports. "It is not that men have an elaborate idea of fatherhood and then don't live up to it," Hochschild explained. "Their idea of fatherhood is embryonic to begin with." The uninvolved fathers had modeled their behavior after their own fathers rather than their wives, mothers, or other men, as had the more involved fathers.

Hochschild's study makes it clear that as more women work, the unfulfilled expectation of shared care is shifted more squarely onto a man's shoulders. Yet, as Dr. A. E. Gottfried and Dr. A. W. Gottfried reported in *Maternal Employment and Children's Development* (1988), on average fathers spend twenty-six minutes a day engaged in direct interactions with their preschoolers. Above the age of six, that decreases to only sixteen minutes daily.

Why don't men participate? Perhaps, as Dr. Louise B.

Silverstein of New York University suggested in the October 1991 *American Psychologist,* the resolution of the dilemma is difficult because the choices are seen as untenable: Either the father must share in the work load and "deal with his own anxiety that these tasks are not included in his definition of manhood," or he withdraws and then must "steel himself against his wife's resentment and generate rationalizations that explain his privileged status within the family." In either case, marital tensions heighten. (Silverstein theorized that the solution lies in including and valuing nurturing and attachment in our definition of what it means to be a man.)

Moreover, a 1987 study by R. C. Barnett and G. K. Baruch published in the *Journal of Marriage and the Family* shows that men with "traditional" orientations (those who believe child care is a woman's domain) who do get involved may not be happy about it. These researchers found that traditional men in dual-wage families are less satisfied with their marriages than those who are the sole breadwinners. They theorize that men in single-wage families participate with their kids because they choose to do so, while in dual-wage families a father's involvement is predicated on the number of hours his wife works.

Some men may resent the new role that has been "foisted" upon them and may fear that their careers are suffering as a result. As E. Anthony Rotundo of Phillips Academy asserted in an article published in the *American Behavioral Scientist,* "One can safely guess that there are more *women* who *advocate* Androgynous Fatherhood [where men share in traditionally female chores] than there are *men* who *practice* it." For some men, the burden of responsibility for child care and household tasks takes some of the fun out of their interaction with their kids. It can feel less enjoyable than the internally motivated play single-wage fathers engage in.

The fact that women are employed outside the home does relieve some of the financial burden, making it possible for men to consider cutting back on their work hours so that they can pitch in with the kids. They may dream of assuming more responsibility out of compassion, or a sense of responsibility. But do they? On the whole, the answer is no. If anything, after the birth of a child, today's fathers may work even more.

The Social Context from a Man's Perspective

Dr. Robert S. Weiss, a sociology professor at the University of Massachusetts in Boston and the director of the Work and Family Research Unit, explains why men have continued in their traditional work roles in *Staying the Course: The Emotional and Social Lives of Men Who Do Well at Work.*

Between 1983 and 1987, Weiss and his research team interviewed forty-three successful middle- to upper-middle-class college-educated men between the ages of thirty-five and fifty-five and twenty of their wives. The in-depth discussions took place over a one- to three-year period. Weiss wanted to learn how these men live right now—their "current emotional and relational lives." Dialogue revolved around issues such as work, marriage, fatherhood, family of origin, social commitments outside family and work, experience with psychotherapy, tension and depression, and life goals.

Weiss arrived at some telling conclusions, especially concerning the primacy of work. He found that employment enables many men to play out a sort of fantasy of heroic accomplishment: they go off to slay dragons and defeat bad guys, avert threats, come through in the clinch, and perform "extraordinary feats of skill" against all odds. Explains Weiss, "These fantasies provide an emotional meaning to men's work that helps sustain their effort."

Work is also a way of leaving our mark; it is a form of immortality. Whether we design cars or cabinets, put together real estate deals or jet plane engines, deliver babies or the mail, we see our efforts as making some difference in the world. In addition, work provides us with a sense of community, social place, internal and external recognition, material rewards, a good reputation, emotional and financial security, and ultimately dignity. (If you have any doubts about this, ask anyone who recently has been fired or laid off.)

The expectation that we will just blithely reduce our commitment to work (whether or not our wives are earning good money) is unrealistic. Indeed, 80 percent of the men in Weiss's interviews, when posed the hypothetical question of how they would proceed if they suddenly inherited enough money to lead a comfortable life without working, answered that they would continue working. It's time to stop feeling guilty about the fact that we derive enjoyment and emotional sustenance from our work.

But, because work is so important to us, Weiss found that it can be a "greedy institution." As he explains, "Men generally give work as much time and energy as it requires—and that can be a very great deal. They work hard not because they are forced to by close supervision but because they want to." This means that the man who decides to come home religiously at dinnertime, regardless of projects left unfinished at the office, flies in the face of convention. He risks the disapproval of his coworkers and superiors.

Other experts in the field of fathering, including Michael Lamb, professor of psychology at the University of Utah, support the assertion that men who are highly involved with their families are viewed as being less committed to work and less serious, a perception that threatens their careers. Powerful forces keep us bound to the status quo.

There is an additional conundrum. According to Weiss, work is so important because it provides the foundation for the rest of a man's life. But what if an all-consuming involvement in work prevents a man from functioning as a father and husband? Does that not defeat the purpose?

Weiss writes that the birth of a child justifies a man's life even more than his work does. "Having children helps to make sense out of work, because work now becomes a means for providing for the children. . . . men believe their work is a way of caring for their children." Yet Weiss also finds that despite relative symmetry in modern marriages before the birth of a child, afterwards the old sexual division of labor reemerges: the mother becomes the nurturer, while the father provides financial support for the family.

The mother is emotionally linked to a baby that recently emerged from her, with whose bodily rhythms hers are attuned. The father, in response, is likely to see mother and baby as a unit. A father may feel left out, or he may feel gratified that his wife is devoted to his child, or both. Whatever his reaction, he is likely to feel that his primary contribution to his family will be through his effectiveness in his work outside the home.

Other researchers agree. For instance, Dr. Frances K. Grossman, professor of psychology at Boston University, and her colleagues researched how parents promote autonomy (independence) and affiliation (closeness) in their firstborn children. Their study, published in 1987 in the journal *Family Relations,* describes how even during pregnancy new fathers may devote additional time to work and less to the family. "Many men awaiting the birth of their first child," Grossman writes, "feel compelled to work more hours in order to earn more money, to fulfill their inner concept of a good father."

"New" Fatherhood Requires "New" Motherhood

Other double messages confuse the "new" father. While equity in family responsibilities can enhance a marriage, research has shown that some women feel ambivalent about their spouses' increasing involvement in parenting. They may experience difficulty sharing child care duties, even though they express the wish that the men help. This ambivalence can translate into the mother's hovering over the changing table, giving advice on how to play with the baby properly, or criticizing how the father administers the bottle. Veiled or overt reproaches like these can make a father feel inadequate, subordinate, and ultimately resentful.

Why do mothers act this way? According to Dr. Graeme Russell and Dr. Norma Radin, a woman may feel threatened by her husband's presence in the nursery, as if the man were infringing on the woman's exclusive domain of child care and housework. This may come from a woman's sense of insecurity about her new role as mother, or her need to be "supermom," especially with a first child. In her article, Dr. Grossman explains that a woman may feel guilty and inadequate unless she is the perfect mother and meets all of the child's needs.

A woman who is extremely warm and connected to her child, and who is always the first to respond when the child is in distress, may seem like a great mom, but in actuality she may be monopolizing the parent-child relationship. Her total involvement can preempt the possibility of any close contact between father and child. "If a woman is always warm and empathic, always available to the child," Grossman writes, "her husband is less likely to warmly respond to that child." How can he? He has no opportunity to do so. He feels shut out and perhaps even jealous.

If this is the situation in your home, it would be helpful to engage in a dialogue with your spouse on giving you space to be a father, imperfect as your fledgling attempts may be. This may be a loaded topic, however, since your wife may experience tremendous social pressure to be the main caregiver despite her wish that you participate in parenting with her. You can begin by asking (in a nonthreatening and nonaccusatory way) if it's okay for you to point out when you feel preempted around the kids. Once you identify and agree upon the situations, you can better deal with them. By increasing awareness, you better appreciate choices and open yourselves to the possibility of changing behavior.

A couple came to me for counseling because of a conflict over proper parenting procedures. Both were lawyers and each had cogent and convincing arguments for doing things his or her own way.

In particular, Tom was irritated when his wife, Nancy, reminded him to "be sure to tuck the diaper in so it won't leak." Tom felt that Nancy was constantly elbowing into his relationship with ten-month-old Emily. Couldn't she just let him do it his way? Nancy, on the other hand, expressed her desire to do things "right" with their first child. She feared making mistakes.

I explained that a child can thrive if tasks are approached in more than one way and will probably even benefit by becoming more adaptable. Nancy needed to let go of her fears and trust that Tom was competent, even if his style differed from hers. "So what if the diaper leaks?" I said. "Tom will have to deal with the consequences. And next time, he may be more careful about loose ends—or he may not. Maybe he even enjoys changing Emily frequently."

"Yeah," Tom nodded, smiling. "That's one of the best times for us to play."

I call this approach *parallel parenting*—each parent gets to do it in his way when he's responsible. After all, you and your spouse only want what's best for your family. Parallel parenting becomes a part of the natural process of negotiation that goes on in all families.

In the long run, the whole family will benefit. A 1982 study by Dr. R. C. Kessler and Dr. J. A. McRae, Jr., published in *American Psychological Review* found that when fathers share child care responsibilities, their wives feel less of the strain of the "second shift" and consequently their mental health is enhanced. So is overall marital satisfaction.

Involvement Can Mean Increased Tension with Your Children

Several research studies have reported that fathers' greater involvement with their children can heighten tensions between them. It seems that men who are more active with their kids experience parent-child conflicts similar to their wives' constant day-in, day-out child-rearing headaches. In addition, involved fathers are more likely to feel impatient with their youngsters (a complaint often voiced by women) than are more passive fathers.

But don't let this stop you! The rewards are worth it. The parents in these studies felt that the father-child relationships were more realistic as a result of the men's involvement. Fathers had a better understanding of their youngsters' capabilities and limitations, and their expectations were more accurate. The children could see the patient and impatient aspects of their dads. In Dr. Graeme Russell's study on paternal involvement, the wives viewed these conflicts as a positive change associated with their husbands' increased commitment to child rearing perhaps because they had more compassion for each other and shared experiences.

If you are faced with increased parent-child conflict because you have become more active, you should anticipate a period of adjustment. You may encounter power struggles, balkiness, and school problems. Don't let the inevitable squabbles frustrate you or lead you to believe that you're just not cut out to handle kids. Call upon your own memories in dealing with these experiences and share stories from your childhood (see Chapter 10). Chapter 6 will show you how to discipline authoritatively and set limits with love. Besides, some familial discord is a natural consequence of being a parent and may persist as your children grow.

Other Factors Influencing Your Involvement

The following factors may influence your involvement in child care:

• *Your psychological health:* If you're depressed, anxious, or angry, you may feel less inclined to play with your children. Or your interactions may be less supportive.

• *Your sex role identification:* If you see the father's role in strictly traditional terms (father as disciplinarian and perhaps sports coach), you will severely limit available parenting activities. Feeding the baby, for instance, doesn't fall into either category. Indeed, cultural stereotypes for men don't include child care; there are few role models of participant fathers.

• *Your beliefs:* According to Dr. Graeme Russell, fathers believe more strongly in the existence of a "maternal instinct" (mothers' inborn predisposition to parenting) than mothers do. Men also contend that fathers don't have the same capacity to nurture; consequently, they see children as being better off with their moms. Russell found that the less strongly a man held these beliefs, the more likely he was to participate in parenting (see Chapter 3).

• *Your relationship to your father and the way you were raised:* If your father was available and nurturing, you are likely to be that way with your children. If your father, however, spent little time with you, you may feel the need to make a correction with your own children (see Chapter 4).

In a 1981 study published in the *Merrill-Palmer Quarterly,* Dr. Norma Radin of the University of Michigan found that involved fathers were more often partners in marriages in which both spouses had grown up in dual-career families. Perhaps these couples were accustomed to the idea of dad pitching in at home.

• *Your self-confidence:* Weiss's and Grossman's research demonstrates that a man who feels good about himself conveys this emotion to his children in constructive ways. Conversely, if a man lacks confidence, he may communicate his negative feelings. In addition, a confident man may feel secure enough to abandon traditional sex-role stereotypes.

• *Quality of the marriage:* This is a complex area. As discussed earlier, your wife's conscious and unconscious attitudes may indirectly affect how you perceive your role as father. Grossman also found that the more adept mothers were at parenting, the better fathers were at it, too. She surmised that these better-equipped dads learned parenting skills from their spouses.

• *Your age:* This may affect the amount of time you feel you can devote to your family. Men in their thirties, the prime years for career advancement, may feel obligated to work longer hours than men in their twenties or middle forties. (The greatest work effort is often necessary at precisely the time your family needs you the most.)

• *Socioeconomic status:* In a second study published in 1988, Grossman found the higher a man's socioeconomic status, the better he feels about himself, the more satisfied he is with his marriage, and the more nurture and cognitive stimulation he provides his children.

• *Your wife's age, job status, and autonomy:* In Grossman's later study, husbands of wives who were older or more autonomous or held higher occupational status spent less time with their children. Grossman speculates that these fathers feel confident that their wives can handle parenting adequately on their own.

• *Your child's personality and character:* Children aren't always chips off the old block. You may feel put off by an introverted child if you are an extrovert or by an athletic child if you prefer intellectual pursuits.

• *Your child's gender:* Men tend to spend more time with their sons than with their daughters (see Chapter 5).

Use Family Negotiation to Resolve the Dilemma

For all social changes, new attitudes always precede new behaviors. Fathering is no exception: most of us have the desire but haven't yet made the move. Indeed, as a culture, we are on the cusp of two divergent ideas of fatherhood: the traditional all-work, no-diapers dads of our childhoods and the sensitive, involved, caregiving "androgynous" father of our (and our wives') fantasies.

For some, fathering has come to mean doing tasks previously reserved for stay-at-home mothers: cooking, cleaning, bathing, tutoring. If the activities of fathering are reduced to drudgery, however, without the awareness that your involvement with your children can enhance intimacy and eventually have a positive effect on your youngsters' growth and development and your own good feelings about yourself, then fathering for you will become simply an extra and most likely unwelcome chore.

Rather, it's important to remember that your participation in the family enhances closeness with your kids and increases your enjoyment of your role while it helps your youngsters be more successful in school, in relationships with their friends, and in their own adjustment to being male or female. There is everything to gain and nothing to lose in finding time for fathering; it's only a matter of fine-tuning your approach.

It helps to see the business of life as connected to your family as well as your employment. All marriages, like jobs, are alliances in which labor is divided, sometimes along traditional lines. You can use the skills of openness and flexibility in working with your wife for the good of the family. If neither of you is thrilled about changing a smelly diaper, for instance, why not take turns? If someone has to leave work early to pick up a sick child, decide which one by asking yourselves these questions: Which spouse has the more pressure-filled day? Will a financial loss be incurred? Who had the last sick-child duty? Can you divide the task and make trades? For example, can one of you pick up the child while the other spends the afternoon at home with her with the promise to reverse roles the next time the flu strikes?

Each family must set its own parameters for the father's participation. While it would be inappropriate if not impossible for me to create solutions to your own family's dilemma, the most straightforward technique is to list, prioritize, and schedule parenting tasks appropriate for sharing, such as bathing the baby, helping with homework, dropping off at day care, preparing for bedtime, or coaching the soccer team. Each of you then has the opportunity to choose favorite activities, while the less enjoyable tasks are divided equitably. You might even want to set up a weekly calendar of involvements, charting your parenting activities for the sake of clarity until they become routine. Remember to be flexible and to plan for trade-off and further negotiation as the situation warrants. Your plan may change as your family needs change.

Some days one of you may do more than the other, but on the whole, try to negotiate stability into the arrangement. Maybe a 50–50 arrangement is impossible in your family. A more realistic 65–35 split (your share being the smaller one) may be all that you can muster. That may still be worthwhile, since even a 10 percent increase in your involvement may create a 50 percent improvement in the quality of your relationship with your kids.

If your children are old enough (by the age of five, for sure), they'll want and need to be included in your plan, since they may have their own ideas about how and with whom they want a task done. If you and your wife are trading roles, it's important to let your children know in advance that from now on things will be done a bit differently in the family: you'll be reading the bedtime stories and taking them to the doctor, whereas now she'll coach the team and drive them to school. These changes and negotiations also provide a great opportunity to teach your youngsters flexibility and nontraditional roles.

If conflicts arise over work, household chores, and leisure time, try a time-use schedule that graphically depicts what you and your spouse's days are like. Using a bar graph or even a blank appointment calendar, log how many hours each of you spends per week at work, at household chores, in unstructured leisure, at community or extended family involvements, and with the kids. A chart has the quality of being "objective." From that common ground, you and your wife can enter into a more conscious negotiation about trading off blocks of time in which you're each available.

Whether or not you record your new arrangements is up to you. For some couples, written "contracts" are best. For others, informal agreements work just fine. If you find yourselves slipping back into old patterns, however, it may help to write down your respective commitments so that you both have the same point of reference.

Exactly what requires negotiation may depend on your financial and time limitations. If you find yourselves in conflict, try to deal with one issue at a time; the shotgun approach will only serve to confuse you. In weighing whose day has greater "value" (and so should be left undisturbed), you may have to account for family needs. Some couples can ill afford the highest earner to take time off from work to babysit a sick child. For others, financial issues are less relevant than business deadlines or demanding, unsympathetic bosses.

Bear in mind that your increased participation may temporarily unbalance previously accepted roles. It's wise to anticipate an adjustment period as you and your wife learn how to accommodate the new arrangement. There is no simple way to resolve these inevitable conflicts. Perhaps it's best to perceive them as challenges to come up with new solutions. Conflict in itself isn't bad—it's a useful part of changing ingrained attitudes. Keep motivation high by remembering that this negotiation can resolve family disparities and improve every aspect of your relationship with your kids. Your overriding concern should be their well-being.

Believe that the solution to the "new" father's dilemma lies in establishing a climate of fairness in the family. Following the research and guidelines in this chapter, recognize the contradictory pressures that you and your wife have been experiencing and reflect on how these pressures influence your own decisions vis-à-vis your family. I have found that for many couples, the subliminal pulls of our shifting cultural values underlie most conflicts over work and family involvement.

It's also essential to become conscious of your own assumptions. One father, the manager of a car repair shop, claimed to be totally involved with his son. Yet a blank stare was his only response to my question, "Great! How often do you get up at night to feed him?" Why should his wife always have to do the 2 A.M. feeding? She works, too.

Appreciate your wife's work outside the home. Avoid valuing it only according to the amount of money she makes. Lamentably, women still do not have equal earning power. Whether your wife contributes 60 percent of the household income or 10 percent, her work is just as important to her as yours is to you and deserves your respect.

Finally, our wives also need to change. Some women may

have to loosen their hold on the parenting reins if they wish their husbands to participate more. This, too, may be the subject of family negotiations. But first, you have to become aware of and discuss your family's interaction patterns using the negotiating style I've recommended.

The way that you choose to resolve your "new" father's dilemma will have a dramatic impact on your children. Youngsters often learn vicariously, by observing adults. Your quest for equity in your relationship will influence how your kids ultimately view their own roles as father and mother. The changes you make today can affect generations to come.

3

Can Fathers Nurture?

MEN desperately want to relate to their children, but sometimes they buy into the illusion that being a nurturing father means acting exactly like a mother. That, of course, is impossible: fathering is different from mothering. Yet the persistence of this illusion leaves many men at a loss. Actually, this can be an advantage. Because dads aren't moms, they bring something different—and equally valuable—to the family.

This point was brought home in a Finding Time for Fathering workshop. Steve had come to the class because he was in the throes of a dispute with his wife. Steve liked to get down on the floor and let three-year-old Jessica climb all over him. This usually resulted in an all-out tickle war/ mini-wrestling match followed by paroxysms of giggling and ultimately exhaustion. If Norma was home, she hovered over their play, wringing her hands and gasping in fear at every thump and shriek. Norma's anxiety caused Jessica to stop playing and look at her mom. "It breaks the flow of our game," Steve complained to the group. "I get irritated at my wife and start yelling at her to leave us alone. 'I'm not doing anything wrong,' I tell her. 'I'm not hurting her.' But that only makes it worse; Jessica and I end up feeling frustrated and angry."

Norma insisted that Steve's kind of play was too rowdy, that their daughter would get hurt. Instead she wanted Steve to read to Jessica or help her do puzzles. Of course, Steve had no objections to these activities, but he also wanted to have fun with her and tussling on the floor was terrific fun. Jessica certainly didn't seem to mind. Yet Norma had sown the seed of doubt.

The group responded enthusiastically to Steve's concerns. Some of the other men recalled a similar reaction from their wives about physical play. However, these men were able to convince their spouses that roughhousing (except with infants, whose brains are easily bruised) was an acceptable form of interaction. Other men's wives actually encouraged such rough-and-tumble. Interestingly, all of the men played with their children in the same manner. This reassured Steve, who realized that his wife had simply suggested ways to play that felt familiar to her.

Steve's question echoed a concern of many men. They often feel pressure from their wives or from society at large to be gentle, to engage in quiet activities with their children, or to approach activities in a calm, "cuddly" way. Yet traditionally physical "male" activities such as tag, hide-and-seek, sports, and piggyback rides are naturally part of the bonding process. Even the way men carry their kids off to bed or administer discipline is often playfully physical.

Your Distinctive Contribution

As University of Utah psychologist Michael Lamb puts it, "Fathers are not merely occasional mother-substitutes: they interact with their infants in a unique and differentiable way." Whereas mothers tend to talk to or cuddle with their kids or play with dolls, blocks, and puzzles, fathers naturally engage in physical activities such as roughhousing or made-up games like Sock Wars (who can score more points by hitting his opponent with rolled-up pairs of socks), tag, making funny faces, hide-and-seek, or sports.

As a result of these different playing styles, children often look to their mothers for warmth, quiet-time activities, and verbal stimulation, while they value their fathers as wonderful playmates who introduce them to the world at large. Both are important.

In a carefully structured investigation at Yale University, Dr. K. Alison Clarke-Stewart found that many children prefer to play with their dads. Clarke-Stewart wrote that eight of the fourteen toddlers involved in her research "consistently chose to play with father first and displayed a stronger preference for him as a playmate." She attributed this not so much to a preference for the person, but rather to a preference for what men had to offer. Father-play tends to be lively, unpredictable, creative, imaginative, and obviously exciting. Fathers also naturally interact with their children in short energized bursts, somewhat like the great teacher who has learned to leave his students on a high note so that they're eager for more interaction the next time around.

Children are attuned to the differences between paternal and maternal interactions as early as two weeks of age. Dr.

T. Berry Brazelton, the well-known child care expert and professor of pediatrics at Harvard University, was among the first researchers to recognize that when he hears his father's voice, a newborn's "face elongates, his shoulders bunch, his eyebrows shoot up, he becomes still with anticipation—all signs he is expecting some excitement."

Not only are these differences normal, they are crucial to a child's development. Each parenting style teaches your child different things about the world. Mother's approach informs him that the world can be cuddly, safe, nurturing, and supportive. Father's process lets him know that it can be all of those things but also jostling, unsettling, fun, and surprising. According to Brazelton, "Each parent offers an entirely different outlet for the baby, and so each fosters a different side of the baby's personality."

It is important to realize that your male style of nurture is distinctive and valuable even if it's less validated in our culture. You don't have to feel guilty, as Steve did, for doing what comes naturally. Not only are you not doing anything wrong, you are offering your child something priceless.

The Scope of Male Nurturance

As you can see, the issue is not whether we men can be nurturers—it's obvious that we can and that our children love us for it—but rather, whether we will allow ourselves to appreciate our unique nurturing capabilities and use them to enhance our children's growth and development.

First, let's define male nurture more fully. Society's notions about nurture are often limited to such activities as cuddling, nursing and diapering, and comforting. While men can participate successfully in all but the breastfeeding, they often fail to take adequately into account what nurture really consists of. In fact, it includes much behavior that differs from women's, but nurtures nonetheless.

In the most general sense, when we nurture, we promote the growth and development of an inanimate or animate object (an idea, a business, an athletic skill, a garden, a coin collection, a relationship, a child) by providing the protection, nourishment, care, support, guidance, and encouragement that will allow that object to reach its potential. We may nurture out of self-interest (for example, we stand to gain if our new business prospers) or simply out of love and concern, like that we feel for a baby.

Over a lifetime, we may choose to nurture many different people and things in a variety of ways. But when we become parents, we feel especially drawn to nurturing our children. Their nurture can take several forms:

• We may become involved by setting limits and providing discipline, offering guidance, correcting our youngsters' errors in judgment, and teaching values.
• We may take responsibility for our children's physical care—the feeding, bathing, dressing, bottle-washing, hair-combing, and doctor-visiting aspects of parenting. We may have sole charge of these activities for short or extended periods of time.
• We may take responsibility for socializing our children by teaching them how to play games, express their emotions, refrain from violence, cover their mouths when they cough, win or lose competitions with decorum, and get along well with others (see Chapter

5). Discussions and follow-ups with teachers and school administrators about our children's progress are also part of this process.

• We may make decisions that will affect our children's future, such as which schools and camps they will attend, what form of religious observance the family will follow, what level of income the family will attain, and where the family will live.

• We may make ourselves available during a portion of our children's waking hours. The more time we are available, the greater the potential for interactions. (A caveat here: Simply being around the house helps your children learn—they model themselves after you—but it isn't the same as direct interaction. Watching the ballgame alone on Sunday afternoon is not a substitute for doing something with your kids. You've got to be willing as well as physically present. On the other hand, if both you and the kids enjoy the sport, you can watch together and comment on the game's progress. That's a source of interactive fun and can be nurturing.)

• We are our children's first and best playmates and their favorite bedtime-story readers.

As fathers we can express warmth and comfort our children when they are upset. We can encourage autonomy by praising their independent problem solving. We can hug and kiss. All this is nurture.

All men are good at some of these activities (and no one, male or female, is good at all of them). Each activity constitutes nurturance, and any will benefit both fathers and children.

Reclaiming Your Equal Capacity to Nurture

Even though we are nurturers, we often don't think of ourselves as such because from earliest childhood onward, society doesn't teach or encourage us to do so. In order for us to take charge of our male nurturing capacities, we may first have to overcome strongly ingrained social conditioning. The truth is, a young boy's ability to nurture is not reinforced in our culture. As Dr. S. L. Bem, an expert on sex roles, wrote in 1983, "Adults in the child's world rarely notice or remark upon how strong a little girl is or how nurturant a little boy is becoming, despite their readiness to note precisely these attributes in the 'appropriate' sex."

Dr. Alan Fogel and Dr. Gail F. Melson of the Department of Child Development at Purdue University and Dr. Jayanthi Mistry of the University of Utah studied sex differences in nurturant behavior. In an article published in the book *Origins of Nurturance,* they theorized that boys and girls are equally capable of nurturing but respond differently because of social learning. The researchers cited studies in which school-age boys and girls (and their parents) had identical physical responses (heart rate and galvanic skin response, measures of anxiety) to pictures and recordings of babies crying. These were universally upsetting. Other studies of older siblings responding to younger siblings at home showed few sex differences, except that boys gravitated to male babies and girls to female babies.

After interviewing young children between the ages of two and eight, Fogel, Melson, and Mistry determined that "boys and girls did not differ in their knowledge about infant characteristics or their ideas concerning the ways different caregivers might nurture an infant. Both sexes expressed equal readiness to care for an infant themselves."

These boys and girls shared the ability to nurture and respond to infants equally. After the age of seven, however, girls show more interest in infants, but boys don't lose their capacity to nurture. They may turn this kind of behavior toward other activities, such as involvement with pets, sports, hobbies, and eventually cars. They do, however, move away from forms of nurturing typically defined as female, such as combing, dressing, or bathing babies. Other studies have suggested that boys express an interest in nurture by being "helpful," "protective," and "watchful," rather than by participating in direct care.

The Early Roots of Sex Roles

Where do these divergent male and female sex roles come from? That's hard to say. Sex roles seem to be a combination of biological determinants and social imperatives. While research has documented that early on, girls and boys exhibit different capabilities (baby girls, for instance, are more sensitive to sound and more verbally adept, whereas infant boys are more active and more responsive to physical stimulation), it is difficult if not impossible to determine which aspects of behavior are inborn and which are learned. Children learn how boys and girls "should" act from the way their parents, caregivers, and teachers treat them; by observation of adult behavior; and through peer pressure and television.

What happens at age six that so drastically changes boys'

behavior? In truth, the seeds for the divergence of sex roles are planted long before school age. In fact, parents unconsciously treat their male and female newborns differently. For instance, Dr. Lori A. Roggman of the University of Arkansas and Dr. J. Craig Peery of Brigham Young University studied play interactions among twenty firstborn four-month-olds and their parents. The researchers found that the amount of time parents spent touching and gazing at their infants (and the babies' return gaze) was influenced by the parent's and the child's gender. In particular, fathers touched their sons more than their daughters. In turn, boy infants gazed at their dads more than their moms. Roggman and Peery concluded that the sex differences in parent-infant play "represent the clear potential for differential socialization of males and females by both fathers and mothers in the first few months of life."

Other researchers have found similar subtle differences. For instance, in a 1989 article published in the journal *Sex Roles,* the research team of Alyson Burns, G. Mitchell, and Stephanie Obradovich explained that girl infants are more likely to be carried or pushed in strollers, whereas boy infants are allowed to walk freely more frequently. In 1984, Dr. R. Stewart and Dr. R. Marvin reported that caregivers were more likely to respond to the needs of female infants than male infants. Moreover, Michael Lamb of the University of Utah in a 1980 study discovered that mothers held their children more to perform caretaking functions and to restrict them (as a form of discipline), whereas fathers held their children more to play.

In all of these and a myriad of other subtle interactions, we consciously and unconsciously teach our sons to be physically active and "strong" while conveying to our daughters a sense of openness and "availability." Most of us believe that boys and girls are actually born with different capacities to nurture, though most experts in the field feel it is not so. In a 1990 article on gender and relationships, the noted Stanford University developmental psychologist Eleanor Maccoby explains that when children are observed individually, boys behave much like girls. Differences in behavior gender boundaries emerge only when the children are put into mixed gender social situations.

Indeed, as Carol Nagy Jacklin, a psychology professor at the University of Southern California, points out in a 1989 article published in *American Psychologist*, young children know more about their own sex-appropriate behavior and attitudes at much earlier ages than we have any reason to believe they should. Jacklin and Maccoby have shown in earlier studies that children as young as thirty-three months are already aware of gender differences and are distrustful of members of the opposite sex.

How Sex Roles Solidify

As early as thirty-three months, children prefer same-sex playmates. After observing 100 preschoolers on school playgrounds, Maccoby and Jacklin found that four-and-a-half-year-olds spend three times as much time with same-sex playmates as they do with those of the opposite sex, even when activities are gender neutral, such as riding Big Wheels, climbing on a jungle gym, or using finger paints. By the time youngsters reach the age of six and a half, they spend eleven times as much time with same-sex friends.

This gender segregation occurs because boys and girls

have radically different play styles, perhaps stemming from disparate socialization during infancy and toddlerhood. The rough-and-tumble games in which school-age boys most frequently engage are oriented toward competition, dominance, and one-upmanship. Boys play in large groups, usually in streets and public parks. Mutual interests such as sports bring them together. Such play is distasteful to girls, who prefer intimacy and reciprocity. Girls play in homes and backyards with two or three close friends, where they form intimate bonds, share secrets, collaborate in making up games, and enjoy deep emotional ties.

Interestingly, Maccoby found that girls have a hard time influencing boys (say, to stop bothering them) by using typically polite suggestions, whereas boys will change their behavior if other boys (but not girls) order them to do so. It is Maccoby's theory that girls (just like the rest of us) are not inclined to interact with people who don't respond to them and so begin to avoid boys.

The net effect of these highly segregated play groups during middle childhood is that they create "powerful socializing environments" in which boys and girls become differently acculturated. Indeed, it is Maccoby's belief that boys and girls grow up in essentially different worlds.

It is during this period that male and female sex role behaviors become solidified into the distinctive patterns that we recognize in adults. Maccoby emphasizes the importance of the all-male peer group as the setting in which "boys first discover the requirements of maintaining one's status in the male hierarchy." From earliest childhood onward, those requirements have had little to do with nurture.

What goes on in boys' peer groups? Mostly, boys rehearse being "strong" competitors—perhaps as preparation for their adult lives. In *Staying the Course,* Dr. Robert Weiss describes how school-age boys learn to maintain status in their play environments:

> . . . peers are the most effective teachers of values. Boys slightly older than kindergartners . . . learn from one another, in playground games and in more or less organized sports, to condemn cheaters and showoffs, the clumsy and the incompetent, the cowardly, the egocentric. They learn in confrontations with other small boys to resist aggression, to conquer fear or at least to mask it, to stand up for themselves. In the world of small boys they learn hardihood. They learn not to cry when their feelings are hurt. . . . They learn not to offer alibis for poor performance, not to ask for help. . . . They learn not to talk about their uncertainties and fears except, perhaps, as a means of overcoming them.

After year-in, year-out conditioning such as this, nurturance is eliminated from the repertoire of boys' behavior. It is not reinforced or even held in esteem by other boys.

The More, the Better

Happily, men can and do learn how to nurture once they become fathers. Studies have shown unequivocally that the more time men spend with their babies, the better they become at fathering activities from deftly diapering to the whole range of providing emotional support and direction. This phenomenon is not exclusive to our species alone. In a 1989 article in the *American Psychologist,* Dr. Mary Ainsworth, an award-winning child developmentalist at the University of Virginia, cited research in which even male rats (who, according to Ainsworth, are "conspicuous for the absence of caregiving") did manifest caregiving behavior when confined with newborn rat pups for a sufficient period of time. This suggests that caregiving behavior is likewise innate in male rats, though it's less accessible than in female rats.

Research among human fathers bolsters the view that men can learn to nurture. It is widely known that men present at their children's birth become more involved dads (see Chapter 7). In addition, a 1988 landmark cross-cultural study investigating parenting styles and responsibilities in eleven cultures headed by Dr. B. B. Whiting and Dr. C. P. Edwards concluded that if a man spends time with his infant, the child herself seems to elicit his nurturing response. The child's very presence motivates him to cuddle, smile, and care for her.

Other studies explain why this may occur. In 1988, Dr. Anat Ninio and Dr. Nurith Rinott, child developmentalists at the Hebrew University of Jerusalem, studied 160 Israeli fathers of nine-month-old infants. The researchers measured the amount of time fathers were merely available (in the home during the child's waking hours) versus actually involved in child care, play, or other interactions. They also calculated the daily average number of times fathers fed the child a full meal, dressed or diapered him, bathed him, and put him to bed without a mother's assistance. Finally, they looked at the daily average of how much time the father was solely responsible for his baby.

Ninio and Rinott discovered that fathers who spend no

more than fifteen minutes a day with their infants have exceptionally low (and inaccurate) opinions of what their babies can do. The noninvolved fathers "believe that infants pass the relevant developmental milestones more than three months later on the average than fathers who interact a bit more with their child[ren]." Fathers who interact with their children for an hour or more each day assess the children's social and cognitive maturity more realistically and "generously," and their opinions concur with their wives'.

This is important in several regards. First of all, the operative word here is *interact*. In this study, spending time in the vicinity of the child or mechanically performing caretaking activities was not enough to influence a father's opinion of his child's maturity. Talking, reading, playing, and otherwise interacting with the child made a difference. Second, when a father spends more time with his child, he is more apt to recognize that the youngster is interesting and complex, capable of a certain measure of understanding. This in turn reinforces a father's desire to interact, which can ultimately enhance the child's intellectual development. Children of more highly involved fathers have higher IQ scores (see Chapter 5).

A parent who believes children under fourteen months don't understand picture books won't show such a book to his nine-month-old. Conversely, the greater the level of a dad's interaction, the more accurate his perceptions of his child's development, and the more inclined he will be to provide appropriate intellectual and developmental stimulation. According to Ninio and Rinott, this can create a positive spiral: "Exposing the infant to a cognitively richer diet of experiences is likely to enhance his developmental status." That, in turn, produces a more interesting playmate for Dad.

Attachments and Affiliations

Fathers' psychological and physiological responses to infant cries and smiles are no different than mothers'. Studies have confirmed that given the *opportunity and encouragement,* fathers are just as involved in cuddling, touching, looking at, kissing, and talking to their newborns. (Dr. Ross D. Parke and Dr. Douglas B. Sawin reported in *Psychology Today* that even socioeconomically deprived fathers who have participated neither in childbirth classes nor in the delivery of their babies were just as nurturing as their wives when left alone with the children.) Fathers are also as competent in feeding their infants and measuring the amount of milk consumed. And they are able to decipher a baby's cues like sucking, burping, and coughing. With experience, men become adept at interpreting crying and nonverbal cues.

As fathers we become "attached" to our children even before birth. Since we anticipate nurturing them, we feel invested in their growth and development. We may worry about our pregnant wife's health and diet; we may make sure that she gets enough rest; we interview the ob/gyn; we are thrilled to "see" the fetus on an ultrasound examination and attend childbirth classes with our spouse in preparation for the "big" day.

The birth of the child evokes powerful feelings in both parents. Whereas psychologists often refer to the connection between mother and infant as *bonding,* the father's affiliation with his new child is called *engrossment.* When you become engrossed with your newborn, you

- Feel that your child is beautiful.
- Want to touch and hold the baby.
- Are aware of his or her unique features.
- Express a belief that he or she is perfect.
- Sense that you have fallen in love.

These perceptions are accompanied by a strong attraction to the child and feelings of intense elation at having produced an offspring coupled with the increased self-esteem that accompanies parental pride.

Likewise, children connect with both parents very early in life. Developmental psychologists base the formation of this connection on what is called *attachment theory.* According to this hypothesis, formulated by Dr. J. Bowlby in 1969 and originally based on observations of primate behavior, utterly helpless human infants must use any behavior within their means (such as crying, smiling, or gurgling) to get adults to approach and protect. During the first month or two of life, this behavior is directed toward anyone who is near. As the child matures, however, he begins to recognize primary caregivers, who by the time the child reaches the age of six months have become the child's "attachment figures": they are the ones to whom the infant's "attachment behaviors" (crying, stretching out his hands to be picked up, clinging) are directed when he becomes upset.

Traditionally, developmentalists have believed that mothers are the primary attachment figures. (A one-year-old's protest at being separated from his mother would corroborate this.) Recent research has shown, however, that children approach, touch, and stretch their arms toward their fathers, too. In fact, according to a 1980 study (published in *The Father-Infant Relationship*) by Michael Lamb, a psychologist at the University of Utah and one of the foremost researchers on fathering, babies were equally attached to both parents. In this investigation, there was no evidence to support the popular assumption that infants between the ages of seven and twelve months prefer—or are uniquely attached to—their mothers. Other studies have reported seven-month-old girls being even more attached to their dads than to their moms.

Moreover, Lamb found that boys in particular attached to their fathers, perhaps because men make special efforts to draw their sons' attention. This means that fathers are exceedingly important to their sons from the beginning of the second year of life—not from age four or five, as Freud had proposed.

Along with attachment behaviors, babies engage others in playful interactions. They look, gurgle or talk, smile, laugh, offer toys and cookies, and play. These activities— part of social exchange with friendly people—are called *affiliative behaviors.* Children may engage in affiliative behaviors with their parents (attachment figures) or with friendly strangers.

Interestingly, both Lamb and Dr. K. Alison Clarke-Stewart found that children were significantly more responsive to play initiated by their fathers than their mothers. In Clarke-Stewart's study, children were rated more cooperative, interested, and joyful during play with the father. Furthermore, Lamb ascertained that children engaged in more affiliative behaviors with their dads than with their moms. One-year-olds, for example, smiled, talked, looked at, and laughed with their fathers more than their mothers. Clearly, fathers offer their kids their own brand of nurture.

Work as an Indirect Form of Nurture

In *Raising Your Child to Be a Mensch,* Rabbi Neil Kurshan described a poignant discussion on the conflicting demands of work and family:

> A young man told me of a conversation he had in the hospital with his father just before he died. The father, a perpetually busy man, had not spent much time with his children and the son expressed his regret that they had not shared more together. The father responded by reminding his son that he had worked long hours in order to put food on the table to feed the family. The son remained silent, but in his heart he was yearning to tell his father that he had never been as hungry for food as he had been for his father's presence.

Like this father, you may feel that long hours on the job are justified by the need to sustain the household and provide vacations, orthodontia, and designer sneakers. Your wife's pregnancy and the experience of childbirth may have spurred you to work all the harder, in anticipation of the new responsibilities you were about to shoulder. Ironically, this occurred just when your family needed you most.

My wife saw her dad only on the weekends during her early childhood: he left for work before she awoke and came home in the evening after she was asleep. If your dad kept those long hours, you may feel yourself at a loss to find other ways to nurture your own children beyond the traditional mode of bringing home the bacon.

Take heart: research has shown that fathers' intense *but not exclusive* preoccupation with pursuits outside the home may have some hidden benefits for their children. In a 1988 study by Dr. Frances K. Grossman of Boston University and her colleagues, published in *Developmental Psychology*, it was concluded, among other things, that men's positive involvement in their careers, while shortening the hours that fathers spend with their children, may nevertheless enhance the quality of the father-child interactions, and may even bolster a child's feelings of competence in the world. According to this research team, men who enjoy their work also have sensitive and responsive interactions with their children.

In this study, the men who were most engrossed in their jobs were also the most supportive of close and intimate relationships in their preschoolers. This support enhances a child's sense of self, his ability to make friends and sustain relationships. In addition, men's degree of autonomy (as expressed by work) also predicted which children would be most independent. Perhaps this is because dads who like their work model and encourage particular independence-related traits in their children, such as leadership and decision-making skills. (On the down side, the more a man enjoyed his work, the less time he spent with his family.)

Why is there a positive relationship between work satisfaction and parenting skills? Grossman suggests that a man who is comfortable with himself may be open and willing to learn from his wife. It is also possible, as Dr. Robert

Weiss noted in *Staying the Course,* that a man's on-the-job successes enhance his self-esteem. If a father feels good about himself, his positive self-regard radiates out to members of his family and so his relationship with his children also benefits. It is important to recognize this hidden link between work and fathering: when men are satisfied with their work, they help their children become successful socially and encourage their kids' growing independence.

But despite Grossman's interesting findings, I am not encouraging you to work more. Even an hour a day spent at home instead of at work (reading, playing, storytelling, talking) can make a huge difference in your relationship with your children.

There's certainly nothing unmasculine about changing diapers or giving your infant a bath. Even giving your infant a bottle or otherwise helping out with feedings can be part of your caregiving routine. While overall, masculine and feminine nurturing styles are different, the lines separating one specific activity from another are not so clearly defined. One woman of my acquaintance, for example, explained that her three-year-old son preferred his dad to read bedtime stories, since it provided the point of departure for the kind of imaginative play in which the husband excelled. Similarly, it was the dad in that family who built the castles and zoos out of blocks, thereby engaging the child in a kind of active imaginative play that came more naturally to him than to her.

Your nurture can take any or all of these forms and one response doesn't preclude the others. But however you nurture your family, recognize that you are vitally important to your children's growth and development. Value your unique contributions. Fathering expert Michael

Lamb makes the point that mothers and fathers provide their children with qualitatively different kinds of experience and that their contributions may not necessarily overlap. As workshop participants explained to Steve, the reluctant roughhouser, the nurturance fathers offer their children is stimulating, fun, and exciting to them all.

4

Finding Your Fathering Style: Recapturing the Past

A t a workshop session, Jon talked excitedly about how well he and his dad had gotten along. Jon's father was a natural teacher who enjoyed showing his son how to build a model, how to put together a kite and a bookshelf, how to tune the car engine. As a result, Jon grew up feeling confident and competent in the world of mechanics and decided to pursue engineering as a career. Now Jon wanted to replicate these positive experiences with his own son.

Jon was lucky. Unfortunately, he is also in the minority. Few men in our workshops describe themselves as having been close to their fathers.

Sensing the discomfort of some of the other men in the group whose relationships with their fathers could hardly be described as rosy, I shared an incident that occurred with my dad when I was about nine years old. It, unfortunately, is far more typical.

My father finally agreed to help me fix a flat tire on my bike after a good deal of nagging and whining on my part. We began, happily enough, by collecting all of the necessary paraphernalia: patch, a screwdriver, pliers, a bicycle pump.

Our first task was to get the wheel off the bike. That done, we had to get the tire off the wheel. My father grasped the tire with his left hand. I held the screwdriver wedged between the rubber and rim while he hammered at it, hoping to get the tire to pop off. Suddenly, the screwdriver slipped and jabbed my dad's thumb hard. He threw the wheel down in a rage and stormed into the house, yelling at me for screwing up. The tire was never repaired.

Worse than our ruined time together and the loss of the use of my bike was the blow to my self-esteem. I felt blamed. I felt like a failure. I became afraid to work with my dad and eventually withdrew from him. After that incident, I never felt competent mechanically. To this day, my wife takes charge of the assembly of bookcases, barbecues, and bicycles. She understands that if the project doesn't go perfectly, I get terribly frustrated and down on myself. Even though my mechanical abilities are adequate, I feel as if I'm all thumbs when it comes to fixing things around the house. And there's no way that I could teach these kinds of skills to my daughters.

After I related this story, the room fell silent as we all looked at each other. This moment of introspection was followed by an emotional and personal outpouring.

"My father never praised me," said Michael. "When I brought home an A on a school assignment, he'd ask why I didn't get an A+. He must have lived by the old 'Spare the rod, spoil the child' standard. He thought criticism was the best way to mold my character. Boy, was he ever wrong. It only made me feel like I'd never be good enough to please him—no matter how hard I tried."

"For me," Tom said, "it wasn't the direct criticism. It was the yelling. I couldn't just be told, I had to be screamed at."

"My dad was just the opposite," Dave said. "He'd come into my room and say sternly, 'We have to talk.' But when he sat on my bed, he'd be patient and explain things. At times he lectured too much, but I still felt his caring."

It was clear that our dads still influenced our adult selves. This brought to mind an incident in childhood that eventually affected the direction my life would take.

My father owned and operated a parking lot in downtown Los Angeles. One of the men whom he employed there, Charles, had become a trusted employee, almost a part of the family. Charles had four children and moonlighted on our lot in the evenings after a day job. He was black.

In 1963, when I was about seventeen, my dad bought a new Plymouth Belvedere. He and I were excited and couldn't wait to see the car.

When my father told him about the new Plymouth, Charles decided that he was ready for a new car, too. He asked if my dad could accompany him to the dealership. In 1963 blacks were still openly discriminated against, and Charles feared that he wouldn't get as good a deal without my father's presence.

All went well. Charles ordered a car identical to my dad's and was charged the same price. The situation changed, however, when the cars were delivered. My dad picked his up without a hitch. But when Charles arrived at the lot to take delivery on his, the price went up by $500—no small amount in those days—and Charles could no longer afford the vehicle. He came to my dad, upset and disappointed.

My dad didn't hesitate. He went back to the dealership and told the manager that he would not do business with someone who was dishonest. Either Charles got the car at the price originally agreed upon or my dad was going to return his car, as well. After some hemming and hawing about a "misunderstanding," the manager relented.

I felt really proud of my father. Inspired by his stance and strength, I did my senior project in high school on Jim Crowism, and I participated in Operation Bootstrap after the Watts riots in Los Angeles in 1965. In fact, I worked professionally with minority kids for many years. I felt the need to correct injustices.

Some men are able to transform painful events with their own fathers into happy experiences with their children. Others, unfortunately, try so hard not to be like their dads, they may err in the opposite direction.

Take Tony. His print shop was located in his home. Rather than marking this area as off limits, Tony allowed his son, Mathew, to explore it while under his close supervision. If Mathew took a tumble, Tony would say, "That's okay, Matt, you fell down. You'll be fine." Tony believed that he had created a safe way to allow his son to learn about his environment.

Tony had described his dad as being stern and restrictive, and he was proud of his ability to wrestle with the ghosts of his past. He was immensely excited by the idea that he could give his son permission to experience and explore— permission he'd never gotten from his own father.

Unfortunately, no matter how happy Tony was about the situation, a print shop, with its messy ink and noisy, hot printing presses, is not an appropriate environment for a curious, active preschooler. In trying to undo the damage his father had done, Tony was exposing his son to potential, and perhaps even greater, peril. After our discussion,

Tony recognized the danger and created reasonable limits by setting up a fence so his child couldn't enter the area without him.

Shadowboxing with Our Fathers

In *Finding Our Fathers*, Harvard psychologist Samuel Osherson explains how our relationship with our fathers subtly shapes future responses to our wives and children. "At home some men become determined to avoid the passivity or dependency they saw in their fathers," he writes. "Others feel unable as husbands and fathers themselves to live up to the heroic standards their fathers seemed to set. . . . Many of us strive to be different from our own fathers while also unconsciously trying to live up to their image."

An essential step in understanding the way you influence your children's development is coming to terms with your relationship with your dad. For some men, fathers are obscure figures who spent little time at home. For them, fathering equals providing financially; they have no role model for a more involved type of parenting. For others, fathers were overbearing and restrictive. These men seek to parent their children more democratically and interactively, but they don't know where to begin. Some men have wonderful memories of their dads, but this leads to a different kind of insecurity—wondering if they will ever measure up. Finally, some men can get into competitive shadowboxing with their dads. They become preoccupied with "doing it better," wishing to compensate for deficiencies in their own upbringing, or salving old wounds by aggrandizing themselves at the expense of their admittedly less-than-perfect fathers.

The struggle to define our role as parents involves awkwardness and ambivalence. During parenting interactions our many conflicts manifest themselves as a sort of staccato rhythm of involvement and withdrawal. When realizing that we are repeating our fathers' errors, many of us become anxious and retreat even further. Or we become even more demanding, in an ever-snowballing reenactment of childhood roles.

Feeling unsure about ourselves, we may fear being too involved or not involved enough; too harsh or not firm enough. We hover between the hope that our interactions are effective and valuable and the dread that they are inadequate or harmful. It is important to come to terms with the impact our own fathers have had on our lives in order for us to become more effective, confident, and loving parents.

A Father's Ambivalence

When Bob, a well-respected physician, came into my office, weariness and anxiety were written all over his face. He asked for a pillow to ease the tension in his lower back. Clearly, he was troubled.

"I don't know what I'm doing wrong," he explained. "I love my son. I really want to spend time with him. But when I come home from work, I'm so tired. I need to relax. And if Scotty interrupts me or wants to play, I just lose it. I know

I should be more patient with him. After all, he's only four. But I just can't help myself."

Bob's own father—a physician, too—had worked sixty to eighty hours a week and was too exhausted when he came home at night to cope with the family. As a result, Bob had felt starved for his dad's attention and affection. He recalled being content simply to be in the same room with his dad. There were times when the doting son couldn't help but touch his father's papers and the "important" things on his desk—it was a way to make contact, however limited. His dad became enraged at these transgressions.

No wonder Bob felt trapped. He was shocked and pained when he recognized the pattern he was re-creating, yet he lacked a more positive role model. Somehow Bob had begun to feel again what he had felt as a child: the important things that dads do don't include their children.

As Chapter 3 explained, nurturing takes many different forms. Besides, few men (or women) can plunge into a game of hide-and-seek with their four-year-old after a long, hard day on the job. Sometimes just being with your kids is enough. You don't have to do anything special to be nurturing. As men, we so often remember our dads as *doing* rather than just *being*. We have come to believe that the measure of ourselves as fathers depends on how many "things"—tasks, games, lessons—we accomplish with our kids. Bob's unrealistic expectations about "quality time" were interfering with his relationship with his son.

All children need and want our attention when they haven't seen us all day. They are eager to relate. If, as in Bob's case, our model of "father" distances us from our children or expects them to understand our needs without our having to understand theirs, we are bound to become embroiled in conflict as soon as we set foot in the door. But why create an either/or situation? If we recognize our parenting patterns and decide to change them, we can make room to relax as well as to have quiet contact with our children.

For instance, Bob could let his little boy snuggle on his lap while he read the newspaper, or they could watch the evening news together. The physical contact might satisfy Scotty's immediate desire for attention while allowing Bob his much-needed "decompression" time. Once Bob became more relaxed, he might feel more amenable to playing games with his son and to break the father-child patterns he'd grown up with.

Reading and watching TV in an affectionate, relaxed, and intimate manner are valuable interactions because they provide warmth and contact while allowing you simply to "be" together. They can substitute for other, more engaging activities, such as coloring together or working on hobbies (see Chapter 10), but don't replace them entirely.

"Reliving" the Past

All of us frequently "relive" our pasts when we become parents. Emotional issues long dormant come suddenly alive. The sight of your wife tenderly suckling your baby, for example, may evoke an ancient feeling of neediness and longing. Such primary emotions may have long been repressed, especially if your dad chided you for acting like a "sissy" when you sought the comfort of your mother's warm embrace. Your five-year-old's struggle to master his two-wheeler can provoke rage, which is often a mask for your hidden resentment of your own failures and your father's impatience with your fledgling attempts at bike riding, roller-skating, or hitting a baseball.

Remembering your relationship with your father can make you aware of the many forces that help shape your attitudes and actions. Try to recall the positive and negative images connected with your dad. A word of caution here: If you find yourself avoiding the following questions or feeling apprehensive about them, acknowledge the possibility that they dredge up memories that are particularly upsetting or too painful to contemplate. Go slowly. Skip the most difficult ones and come back to them later.

Answer the following questions on a sheet of paper. Then go back and answer them again, substituting "you" for "your father," and "your children" for "you."

• How would you characterize your father's involvement with you?

• How much time did your father spend at work?

• How much time did your father spend alone with his children?

• What kinds of activities did you engage in together?

• Was your father passive at home, leaving most of the parenting work to your mother?

• Was your father critical, or accepting and supportive?

• Was your father able to teach you skills that he had mastered?

• Did your father play with you? If so, what kind of play?

• Did you grow up feeling competitive with your father?

• Who was the disciplinarian in the household? How did you feel about the discipline system?

• Was your father strict or permissive?

• Could you confide in your father if you had a problem? Were you willing to seek his advice?
• How would you characterize the relationship between your father and your mother?
• As a child, do you feel that you respected your father for his role in your upbringing? Do you feel the same way now that you have children?

Answering these questions honestly can put into perspective your dad's impact on your view of yourself as a parent. Your thoughts become snapshots of you as a father that can be mounted in a mental scrapbook. They are points of reference, helping you to determine if you parent in the same way or differently from your dad. This questionnaire can also be an opportunity for you and your wife to engage in an open discussion about relationships with your respective fathers and your mutual expectations for your fathering role.

Remember, too, that it is impossible to undo the past. Awareness is just the beginning; it takes a good deal of effort to become a conscious parent. But once you've gained a clear sense of your connection to your dad, you can make some constructive moves. For a more in-depth exploration of these issues, you might want to refer to Sam Osherson's *Finding Our Fathers,* Warren Farrell's *What Men Really Want,* or Robert Bly's *Iron John.* If these issues are exquisitely painful or too difficult to explore honestly alone, a therapist can be helpful.

Making a Change

The simplest approach to finding your fathering style may be creating a two-column list. On the left side of a sheet of paper, record events, interactions, or behaviors that were most disturbing to you during your childhood and now irritate you in your children. On the right, brainstorm a novel approach. If, for instance, your father was always critical, you could try praising your youngsters' efforts rather than the outcome of a task, or looking upon the completion of a project as a series of successive approximations rather than a do-or-die, either-get-it-right-the-first-time-or-don't-bother-with-it-at-all approach. The following is an example of such a list.

EVENT, INTERACTION, BEHAVIOR	POSSIBLE NEW APPROACH
Johnny makes the bed once a week without my having to scream like my dad did.	Set up system of rewards. A point for every made bed. After ten points, a Ninja Turtle reward.
Sally lied about homework to get out of trouble. My father would have spanked me for that.	Talk to Sally about her fears. What prompted her to lie? How is she doing at school? Does she need help? Set up conference with teacher. No need to punish her more. She had to face me and teacher and make up work. Missed movie we planned.

It's best to work on one issue at a time. The scope may range from having your youngster make his bed to raising a moral human being. In fact, it may help you to see that the making of a bed once a week teaches your preschooler responsibility, an important component of accepted moral and social behavior.

Of course, what works on paper doesn't always work in reality. You may have the best intentions but still find yourself slipping back into old patterns when you're feeling tired or impatient. Enlist the help of your children, your wife, even your friends. The following steps may help resolve conflicts that stem from reenacting your past.

1. *Ask for feedback.* In advance, ask your wife, a friend, or a trusted relative to observe and give you feedback about your parenting. Have your helper pay attention to whether the intensity of your response is appropriate. For instance, does your anger at your son's five-minute tardiness at dinner make sense (given that he's chronically late for school, church, and other commitments), or have you built your anger into a rolling boil because of events in your past (say, your father's constant absence at dinnertime) that make your son's infraction seem more serious than it really is?

2. *Give yourself a breather.* You won't respond to your child or to the feedback if you're furious. Take a few minutes to collect yourself before you let everyone have it with both barrels and say hurtful things you'll probably regret later. You can say to a teenager who missed her curfew, "Give me a few minutes. I have to think about an appro-

priate consequence. I don't want to lay the same punishment on you that my father did on me."

3. *Watch for your own defensiveness.* Make sure that your helper knows how to deliver feedback without setting off other internal fireworks. (There's no point in fighting with your wife *and* your son!) In advance, instruct your helper to *mirror* your reactions: she should repeat back to you what she sees without making a value judgment. She could say, "It looks like you're having a hard time handling Marty's losing his math book again. What's going on inside of you? Is your reaction appropriate? Does it recall something in your past?"

4. *Answer honestly.* Admittedly, this is the tough part; few men like to confess mistakes. But now is the time to reflect back on your questionnaire. Is there something in your preschooler's sassing you that triggers an old hurt? If so, acknowledge the connection to yourself, your helper, and, if he's old enough to understand, to your son.

5. *Apologize.* Say, "I'm sorry, kiddo. I blew it. I just found myself getting angry at something that didn't belong to you." Then explain the circumstances of your childhood that gave rise to your strong and perhaps unwarranted reaction. Or, if you've reacted in knee-jerk fashion to an offense in the same way your father used to, you can say, "I'm sorry, kiddo. I overreacted. I just found myself doing to you what my father used to do to me. I hated that as a kid! Can we talk about it?"

If your child is too young to handle this information, talk it over with your wife. If she's unavailable, talk to a close friend. It's important to share your mistakes. No one is perfect (most parents find themselves in the same predicament from time to time); just having the support of others helps to alleviate negative feelings and guilt. Furthermore, speaking up helps to render unconscious motivations and injuries more conscious. And once you are aware of hidden issues, you can take charge of them better and alter your future response.

6. *Express love.* Most people feel cleansed and freed of guilt when they sincerely acknowledge mistakes. In addition, your child or helper will most likely respond with empathy. Everyone can relate to occasional transgressions. Your confession will make you seem more human in your child's eyes (especially since he knows firsthand what it means to be imperfect) and draw your family closer.

Altering how you relate to your family is an act of will that takes courage. You may find yourself facing long-buried grief, anguish, and solitude when you consciously confront your relationship with your father. This is normal. Although painful to experience in the moment, however, you may find that this exercise leads eventually to an enriched and more open and loving relationship with your children.

PART 2

*Your Vital Role
in the Family*

5

What You Have to Offer: Fathers' Impact on Child Development

In a 1984 interview in *Esquire* magazine, Dr. T. Berry Brazelton commented, "Everything we know shows that when men are involved with their children, the children's IQ increases by the time they are six or seven." But perhaps more intriguingly, Dr. Brazelton points out that with the father's involvement "the child is also more likely to have a sense of humor, to develop a sort of inner excitement, to believe in himself or herself, to be more motivated to learn." Clearly, these qualities have a greater impact on a child's future development than IQ alone.

During the last two decades, child developmentalists have spearheaded a quiet explosion of research into the father's impact on child development and have found that different fathering styles can have positive or deleterious effects. While mothers certainly play a role in development, and most interactions with children depend on complex family dynamics, for the purposes of understanding your impact on the family, we are focusing on fathers' contributions. Indeed, much of the research in this new field attempts to isolate fathers' influence as its sole purview. Let's look at the three most salient styles of fatherhood: authoritarian, permissive, and authoritative.

The Authoritarian Father

An authoritarian father treats his children with little respect. He sets down the law and is rigid in his communications. In his mind, there are only two sides to any question, his way and the *wrong* way. He may impose punishments arbitrarily and offer threats such as, "Do it, or else," or "Do it because I told you to."

In a 1990 *American Psychologist* article on drug use and adolescents' mental health, University of California at Berkeley psychologists Jonathan Shedler and Jack Block characterize an authoritarian father as one who:

• Is unresponsive or insensitive to his children's needs.
• Prohibits open disagreement between himself and his children.
• Maintains tight control.
• Is critical of his children and rejects their ideas, suggestions, or originality.
• Discourages his children from becoming independent.
• Is impatient with his children.
• Is overly interested in his children's performance, intrudes physically into their activities, and pressures them to work at tasks.

According to these two researchers, the authoritarian father "does not appear to enjoy being with his child, and he ensures that his child does not enjoy being with him."

By the age of eleven, the children of these fathers tend to be:

- Relatively fearful and anxious.
- Physically inactive; not vital, energetic, or lively.
- Inhibited and constricted; unlikely to compete.
- Fearful of new experiences; lacking in curiosity.
- Looking to adults for direction; unassertive; insecure.
- Unresponsive to humor; cold; shy.
- Immobilized under stress; obedient and compliant.

Some men contend that criticism will toughen their children (particularly their sons) and prepare them for the world, that it's a form of support. They give the example of a beloved coach who whipped the team into shape with harsh words and admonishments. The difference may lie in the fact that the coach focuses on *performance,* whereas fathers tend to zero in on their children as people. Statements like "You're bad," "You're lazy," "You're clumsy" tell your child that she is unworthy as a person. This attitude is often conveyed by body language and tone of voice alone.

In fact, critical fathers are emotionally withholding and nonsupportive. Not surprisingly, their children are more likely to feel rejected and unhappy. According to Dr. Norma Radin of the University of Michigan, studies have demonstrated that distant and authoritarian fathers who criticize their preschool boys tend to hinder their sons' intellectual growth because anxiety is heightened. Research also suggests that the relationships between delinquent boys and their fathers is characterized by hostility and rejection. Investigations into authoritarian fathers' impact on their daughters are sparse, but one can guess that the effects are similar.

In my fathering workshops I often give a graphic demonstration of how authoritarian fathers diminish their children's confidence. I call for a volunteer and ask this brave soul to stand in the middle of the room and raise his arms out to his sides. Then I instruct him to resist me as I try to push his arms down. Believe me, I'm not all that strong and my goal is not to humiliate this man. Usually, in fact, I have little success in getting him to lower his arms.

But then I ask if we could try the same experiment a second time. Only now, I yell, "No! Bad!" while shaking my finger at him before I begin to push his arms. Invariably, my volunteer's arms drop as soon as I exert some downward pressure. I apologize if I've frightened the participant, and sometimes we have to take a moment for him to collect himself—especially if this is the way his father treated him when he was a boy.

This simple demonstration always gives rise to animated discussions. The participants remember such treatment and then painfully admit having related to their own children using force, blame, or ridicule. They get their way with their kids, but at such a price that they ultimately feel defeated.

Authoritarian behavior also causes marital conflict. Women want their husbands to be involved in child rearing—but not in *that* way. Indeed, men themselves feel conflicted when they behave in an authoritarian fashion. They are torn between the image of the father they want to be and the reality they present.

Clearly, criticism does more harm than good. Extremely

dominant fathers stifle their children's competence and independence. Often youngsters respond to authoritarian fathers by taking too much responsibility and blaming themselves inordinately for mistakes common to all kids. These youngsters suffer from lowered self-esteem, a crippling burden throughout life. They may withdraw from their dads in fear, or lash out in rebellious anger at siblings, playmates, pets, even favorite toys.

The Permissive Father

On the opposite end of the spectrum is the permissive father. Rather than establishing arbitrary and inflexible rules, he has difficulty sticking to limits in the face of his child's tears, tantrums, or other manipulations. Unfortunately, such equivocal behavior sends the message that he doesn't mean what he says. When this occurs, youngsters become like the tail wagging the dog. They have learned to ride roughshod over their parents and whoever else will let them, making everyone's lives miserable—including their own.

You can readily recognize these children. Often other kids don't like to play with them because of their constant bullying or whining. They rarely take responsibility for their own misdeeds, making excuses to cover their own deficiencies.

"The dumb teacher didn't explain . . ."

"Billy made me . . ."

"It's not fair!"

"How come Lisa's father buys her . . ."

"All the other kids can . . ."

"Mommy, Daddy won't let me . . ."

All kids may use these expressions, but in permissive families they're effective as manipulations. Indeed, children of permissive parents quickly learn to manipulate others. (Sometimes, for example, it's not a question of fairness, but rather of a bedtime missed, a homework assignment shoddily completed, or three peanut butter cookies snitched before dinner.) When you set reasonable limits, you are actually promoting emotional well-being. All children need structure, routine, and safe boundaries. If your child knows where you stand, he can depend upon it, and even if he's not happy about your position, he will feel more supported and secure than if he perceives that he can push you around.

Although some dads may indulge all of their children, a few believe that they ought to be permissive particularly with daughters. They may fear being cast in the role of "bad guy" when it comes to denying their children's requests. Out of a misguided sense of gallantry or fear of losing their daughters' love, they may respond to the feminine stereotype of the demanding and spoiled "princess," and treat their daughters accordingly. Such role models are woven into our social fabric. Permissiveness can lead to your daughter's becoming a "Daddy's little girl." What's wrong with that? Plenty! Catering to your child's every whim or continually solving her problems for her eventually inhibits her motivation to take charge of her own life. Excessive concern begins to sound like condescension, as if girls were incapable of acting autonomously.

Expressions such as "I know you want me to help you, but let's see how much of this puzzle/math problem/roller-skating you can do by yourself" can go a long way toward encouraging independence. Just like us, kids feel good when they overcome obstacles and accomplish difficult tasks on their own. A reasonable (but not overwhelming) amount of frustration teaches children to persevere when the going gets tough. On the other hand, learned dependency born of your stepping in at the first sign of distress can lead to diminished self-esteem. Your child may come to believe that she'll never color inside the lines or ride a two-wheeler. In fact, she may not if she's been deprived of the opportunity to struggle toward mastery.

Once your "Daddy's little girl" reaches adulthood, she may define herself by the men she's with, always allowing them to "lead" or to take over when she's struggling. That can render her less likely to speak up when she's got an opinion to voice. Such reticence can lead to her feeling victimized in her relationships with men or stymied in her career advancement. Or she may project a distasteful attitude of entitlement—Daddy always gave her what she wanted, so why shouldn't the rest of the world?

Like authoritarian parents, permissive fathers undermine their children's independence and feelings of competence. Youngsters show disrespect for permissive fathers, especially during adolescence, when they may view their dads as weak and easily exploited. As such, permissive fathers make poor role models.

The Authoritative Father

Experts such as Dr. Diana Baumrind of the University of California at Berkeley and Dr. Norma Radin of the University of Michigan point to authoritative parenting as being the most effective approach.

An authoritative father walks the middle ground. He has high standards and rules, yet he expresses a lot of warmth without being overly permissive. He communicates his feelings openly, admits his mistakes tactfully, encourages communication, reasons with his youngsters about family decisions and rules, and responds to their needs. His interactions with his children are characterized by definitiveness and a clarity of limits. He watches out for their welfare and monitors their behavior but does not demand unquestioning obedience. He is challenging without being abrasive, and without undermining his youngsters' self-esteem by being overly critical, impatient, or intrusive. He adapts to their increasing ability and accountability. The authoritative father tempers his interactions with his children with varying degrees of understanding, concern, and empathy.

Empathy is the ability to share in another's emotions. As a father, you express empathy by respecting what your child is experiencing (be it a triumph or a defeat), acknowledging his needs and wants, and showing compassion for his pain. It is the combination of authoritative attitude and empathy that makes for successful fathering.

My daughter Cherie was about five years old when her friend Doug came over to play. Doug lived across the street and was a frequent and welcome visitor. On this particular Saturday afternoon, however, Doug ran into a bit of trouble. He and Cherie were batting a large ball around in the den. Somehow Doug gave it a sharp punch, causing it to careen into the adjacent bathroom, smashing one of the globes of the light fixture over the sink. What a terrible din the glass made as it crashed into the sink and on tile floor!

Upset and frightened, Doug took off in tears. Several minutes later, however, the doorbell rang. There stood Doug, still snuffling and sniffling but tightly gripping the hand of his dad, our neighbor and friend Larry. Larry made no excuses for his son's transgression—both kids knew they weren't supposed to play ball in the house. Nevertheless, he encouraged and supported Doug in making an apology. "Go ahead," Larry coached softly, "don't you have something you want to tell Mitch and Susie?"

After Doug blurted out, "I'm sorry for breaking your lamp," Larry chimed in, "That's good, Doug. That's the way to do it." Larry neither yelled at his son nor made him feel worse than he already felt. Instead, he helped clean up the shattered glass and offered to pay for the breakage. We ordered a new globe for our fixture (we footed the bill since our daughter was also responsible), and when it arrived Doug and Larry ceremoniously returned to our home to screw it in together.

Larry taught his son some important lessons about human nature:

• When you make a mistake, you have to own up to it responsibly.
• People appreciate honesty.
• You feel better about yourself when you resolve a problem.

But Larry also taught Doug some important lessons about Larry. Doug could trust his dad to be fair and understanding; he would hold Doug accountable in a way that did not belittle him. Larry set reasonable standards and expectations while supporting Doug emotionally and with compassion. That's the essence of the authoritative fathering style.

Boys whose fathers are warm, responsive, and nurturing engage less often in disruptive behavior at home and at school. Rather than rendering boys "sissies" (as many of us may have been taught), our affectionate and kindhearted involvement helps our sons to relate positively to their peers and to others in their world.

For instance, if Larry had berated or otherwise humiliated Doug in front of us and our daughter (or even at home, out of our earshot), it's a pretty safe bet that Doug would have been reluctant to come around our house anymore. Moreover, it's also likely that Doug would have been angry at his dad for embarrassing him, which probably would have translated into misbehavior or hostility. If Larry were a stern, authoritarian father, Doug might also have tried to hide the incident from his dad, fearing possible retribution. In that case, Doug's self-esteem would have suffered because of having lied and because the incident would remain unresolved.

On the other hand, if Larry had dismissed the incident or simply focused on Doug's upset feelings, as a permissive father might, the boy would probably have found a way to escape accountability. "It's not my fault, anyway. Cherie should have told me we weren't allowed to play ball in the house."

Authoritative fathers' clear expectations, coupled with

lots of love and warmth, help to draw their children in—kids enjoy being around them. Children trust authoritative fathers because they are dependable, predictable, and consistently fair. Sons especially imitate dads who are nurturant, powerful, and involved in this way.

Because children like and respect fathers who parent authoritatively, these men have a profoundly favorable impact, which reflects most strongly in three critical areas:

• *Socialization:* how well children get along with others in their world.
• *Cognitive or intellectual development:* how well youngsters learn difficult material and do in school.
• *Sex role identification:* how boys and girls see their gender-specific behavior in relation to themselves and to members of the opposite sex.

A child's social, intellectual, and sex role development are central to the formation of personality. Let's look at your influence in greater detail.

How the Authoritative Father Encourages Socialization

Socialization refers to your child's ability to interact with others: to make friends with children of the same or the opposite sex, to accurately read nonverbal cues of teachers and peers (such as knowing when to settle down in class or how to approach new classmates), to control impulsive behavior, to act appropriately, and to feel at ease with you or among other adults. A well-socialized child is a happy child who works and plays well with the people in his world. While all kids have their good and bad days, generally a child who is competent socially:

- Has many friends.
- Is neither too shy nor too aggressive.
- Knows how to cooperate and be flexible: shares materials, time, and space and respects the property of others.
- Is able to correctly assess when and how it's appropriate to join an ongoing game or discussion.
- Responds appropriately to authority figures and peers.
- Is comfortable around children and adults.
- Is able to express his feelings and correctly reads and acknowledges the feelings of others.
- Exhibits empathy at others' distress.
- Is able to get his needs met by using language acceptably (without bullying or whining).
- Makes an effort to abide by the rules and limits of the family and culture and understands right from wrong.
- Is courteous and considerate.
- Feels good about himself and others.
- Can assert himself but can also accept the leadership of others.

Authoritative fathers socialize their children by modeling appropriate behavior. A recent article in the *New York Times* elucidates just how this happens. Columnist Daniel Goleman reported on a new study by Dr. Richard Koestner at McGill University investigating how children develop empathy, one of the most desirable of all social traits.

Dr. Koestner found that the strongest predictor of empathy in adulthood was the amount of time a youngster spent with his father during childhood. He speculated that spending more time with their kids may give fathers "more opportunities to be responsive to their children's emotional needs, and so model empathy for them." Moreover, fathers who are more involved with their kids may be more empathetic to begin with.

Dr. Nancy Eisenberg, a psychologist at Arizona State University, contended in the same article that a parent's empathy for and unconditional acceptance of his children did not in themselves foster children's socially desirable traits. She explained that "warmth alone can encourage selfishness in a child. Children also need a firm hand setting limits and guidelines."

In her study of 127 children, Eisenberg determined that youngsters needed to learn how to give something up and to control their own impulses in order to help others. Parents teach these values by expressing empathy in their interactions with their children and by setting limits. This, in effect, describes the authoritative father.

Many other studies have shown that social competence in boys is directly related to their fathers' affectionate understanding and warm involvement in their lives. Boys emulate their dads. When they reach adulthood, they confirm the effects of the type of fathering they received. For example, in one study college men who scored high on personal adjustment tests perceived their fathers as either highly available (at home a lot) and moderately nurturant (involved in direct, positive interaction) or moderately available and highly nurturant (see Chapter 3). Conversely, in another study men who had trouble making friends reported their fathers to be uninvolved, weak, or neurotic.

Authoritative fathers influence their daughters' social development, too, but with a slightly different spin. Whereas boys benefit socially from fathers who are responsive and nurturant, girls who become socially competent, autonomous, and intrinsically motivated have fathers who are firm and expect age-appropriate responsibility and independence from them. These dads can be demanding and challenging—that is, their parenting style involves lots of fair rules (that are adhered to) coupled with warmth. They provide support along with a call to action. Research suggests that when fathers accentuate the authoritative part of the equation (rules and limits within a context of love) over the empathic side, their daughters will be more socially competent.

How the Authoritative Father Encourages Intellectual Development

Cognitive development, the second sphere of fathers' influence, refers to the flowering of a child's intellectual abilities as reflected in success at school and academic achievement. Psychologists, child developmentalists, and educators have put forth myriad theories explaining how children learn, what constitutes intelligence, and what influences a youngster's ability to absorb difficult material. There is no unified way of looking at these complex issues.

Since a child's intelligence is complex, many factors may influence the ability to learn. These can include the following:

• *Inborn abilities and temperament:* Some children are blessed with innate artistic talent, whereas others are born with superior analytic skills. Genetics plays a role in determining abilities, as does a child's distinct character.

• *Environment:* From birth onward, physical, social, and intellectual stimulation from parents, including one-on-one play, is essential for a child's intellectual development.

• *Socioeconomic background:* Generally, children of economically deprived homes don't do as well in school, most likely because their families lack the wherewithal to provide toys, books, proper nutrition, and time for positive interactions. Children who speak English as a second language are also at a decided disadvantage.

• *Family illness or traumas:* Children of a messy divorce, or those who must cope with the illness or death of a loved one, may be distracted emotionally and so have difficulty concentrating and learning.

• *Physical handicaps:* Youngsters who suffer frequent ear infections during infancy, for instance, may struggle to acquire language skills as toddlers. Learning disabilities, unless detected early, may cripple a child's confidence in school.

• *Self-esteem:* Children who feel good about themselves are more apt to achieve their full potential.

So many factors can affect intellectual development that it becomes difficult to single out fathers' contributions. To say that fathers' involvement with their children absolutely raises youngsters' IQs by a certain number of points may overstate current evidence. Nevertheless, many studies strongly suggest that fathers, particularly authoritative fathers, have positive influence on their kids' thinking styles, intellectual curiosity, and self-esteem. This influence is generally more easily discernable (and therefore studied more thoroughly) among boys than among girls because of the strong father-son bond.

In 1972, Dr. Norma Radin of the University of Michigan completed a study in which she observed forty-two fathers as they interacted with their four-year-old sons. She determined that the preschoolers with higher IQs had more nurturing fathers.

Radin speculated that nurturing behavior motivates a son to identify with his father, incorporate his ideas, and imitate his problem-solving style. A nurturing father may also encourage his child to explore his environment more freely, thus enhancing a youngster's natural curiosity and stimulating his desire to learn about the world around him. Conversely, a more authoritarian approach would inhibit explorations, because it reinforces fear of the unknown.

Other child developmentalists have speculated that, much like socialization, the connection between nurturant fathers and their sons' intellectual success hinges on the ease with which boys can identify with their dads. Similarly, psychologists have found that negative father-son interactions are associated with difficulties in analytic thinking skills and general school achievement. In addition, if fathers become overly involved while their youngsters are learning to master new skills, such as the multiplication tables or the writing of cogent essays, they may interfere in their children's progress. Too much parental attention may hinder the development of an independent analytic thinking style. Perhaps such overinvolvement feels like intrusiveness to the child.

Other factors apply as well. For instance, Ninio and Rinott's investigation of 160 men and their nine-month-old infants (see page 55) indicated that when men spend more time in meaningful interactions with their children, they more correctly assess their kids' intellectual and developmental abilities and are therefore more likely to offer appropriately stimulating play. Highly involved fathers become effective tutors.

Several earlier studies show a correlation between fathers' educational and occupational attainments and their children's intellectual competence: the greater the father's achievements, the greater the children's. Researchers speculate that perhaps the presence of scholarly activity, books, educated visitors, and a father's appropriate involvement in helping his children with academics may be behind this association.

Fathers' effect on their daughters' intellectual development is somewhat more complex and ambiguous. As in the case of social development, the emphasis seems to be not so much on empathy but on expressing expectations in a loving way. Permissiveness seems to blunt girls' academic success, whereas explicit expectations for future achievements have been linked to girls' intellectual accomplishments.

When I give my workshop talks to men accompanied by their wives or to mothers of preschoolers, I do a little informal research. I ask the women in the room to raise their hands if they had a positive relationship with their dads. I then ask those who kept their hands down to tell the group whether they did poorly in math or had math blocks in school. About two-thirds of these women giggle with surprise. How did I know? Conversely, about two-thirds of the hand-raisers did well in math.

My unscientific survey underscores actual research correlations of fathers' presence with higher math achievement in girls, especially if they are available to their daughters between the ages of one and nine. Why does this occur? Analytic thinking style, a typically male way of reasoning, is related to success in math and a facility with spatial relations. Boys develop an analytic thinking style as a result of spending time with their authoritative fathers. It's logical that this would apply to girls, too.

Finally, studies have shown that fathers seem to participate less in their daughters' cognitive development than in their sons'. It has been suggested that fathers have been less concerned with their daughters' intellectual achievements, or perhaps identify less strongly with their girls' successes. Another theory hypothesizes that fathers may express their expectations for their daughters indirectly. They may buy TV sets so their daughters can watch "Sesame Street" or pay for books, special lessons, and tutoring. Dads may also communicate their expectations to their wives, who then exert a direct influence on the girls' achievements. Perhaps as stereotypic roles break down, we will be seeing more fathers encourage their daughters directly.

How the Authoritative Father Influences Sex Role Development

Men have penises and heavy muscle structure; women have uteruses and give birth to babies. That part is easy. But physiology only partially explains our distinctive behavior as men and women. Every society forms certain expectations for each gender—men go off to fight in wars, women keep the home fires burning; men bring home the bacon, women fry it up. These expectations evolve over the millennia and reflect our particular cultural biases, though they are changing.

In our culture, traditionally masculine attributes include assertiveness, ambition, and independence. Sensitivity to others' feelings, the ability to express emotions, warmth, and passivity are considered traditionally feminine attributes. While strongly ingrained in our behavior and attitudes, today these distinctions are beginning to blur. Women, for instance, are fighting for the right to participate in combat, unimaginable during World War II. And men are searching for ways to acknowledge their feelings of compassion and nurturance.

As I discussed in Chapter 3, a child's socialization involves learning—through conscious teaching and unconscious modeling—what behaviors are considered appropriate for his gender. Sex roles refer to behavior that is specific to each gender. Being secure in their sex roles means that your children feel comfortable and happy in their maleness or femaleness, as currently defined by our society.

We used to believe that fathers influenced only their sons' development of masculine gender roles. While it is true that this connection is very strong, current research reveals that fathers have a significant impact on the sex role development of their daughters as well. In fact, developmental psychologists have tied sex role development more closely to fathers than to mothers.

Men tend to be much more interested in the formation

of appropriate sex roles and behavior and tend to have more traditional attitudes about them than women do. Fathers punish what they feel is gender-inappropriate behavior while rewarding appropriate behavior. The differences even come out in play. Fathers play rough-and-tumble games more often with their infant sons, but they cuddle more frequently with their infant daughters. They may substitute "action figures" and toy trucks for their sons' dolls and books. Women tend to differentiate less.

According to Dr. Henry Biller, a psychologist at the University of Rhode Island who has written extensively on sex roles and fathers, "The quality of fathering that the boy receives is generally the most crucial factor in the positive development of himself as a male. . . . If the father is not consistently involved in family functioning, it is much harder for his child to learn to be appropriately assertive, independent, and competent."

The process of sex role identification begins for little boys when they first become aware of how their fathers use the toilet. They realize that both they and their fathers (but not their mothers) have penises and suddenly they want to be "big men," too. This is the initial step in male bonding. As one of the men in my workshop explained, "Whenever Jeffrey heard me in the john, he would drop whatever he was doing, race to the bathroom, and pull down his diaper so he could pretend to pee with me. He still hadn't mastered the art of doing it in the toilet, but he would make a tinkling sound with his mouth as if he meant business!"

Your son mimics you as a way to gain mastery over his world. As he watches how you build a doghouse or toss pancakes, how you assert yourself with your boss or make peace within the family, how you express affection toward your wife or attend to your aging mother, he learns to solve problems your way. In fact, much like the other aspects of his personality, your son's "masculinity" may be directly associated with the amount of time you are available to be imitated. Men unconsciously act on this tendency. Studies have shown that they tend to make themselves more noticeable and attractive to their sons than to their daughters, engaging in more frequent touch and eye contact with them.

Boys begin to prefer their dads as a role model at around two years of age. Researchers have observed nurturing, authoritative fathers rewarding their sons with attention, affection, and praise each time the boys come near. Naturally, the boys then want to spend more time with their dads—time in which to watch and imitate.

As with other areas of development, authoritarian fathers who are restrictive, punitive, and withholding of praise give a boy little incentive for imitation. According to Biller, "The more love and respect the boy has for his father, the more reinforcing his father's approval will be for him." Physical affection such as hugging, hair tussling, and even kissing is key. "Masculine development is facilitated when the father is both masculine and nurturant."

Positive sex role identification has lifelong benefits. Youngsters who are comfortable in their masculinity grow into men who feel confident around women. Several studies have shown that men's adjustment to marriage is associated with their relationship with their fathers as well as the health of their parents' marriage. Of course, fathers also serve as powerful role models in this area. What boys learn vicariously about manhood from watching their fathers interact with their mothers becomes part of their personalities.

Fathers' influence on their daughters' sex role development is quite different. To begin with, girls identify with their mothers when they learn sex roles. For years, however, fathers have encouraged traditionally "feminine" traits, including such clearly negative attributes as passivity and dependency. Today, few fathers would boast about how docile and vulnerable their daughters are! We have come to see that well-adjusted girls and boys are a mix of both traditionally feminine characteristics, such as sensitivity to others' feelings, warmth, and the ability to express emotions, and more "masculine" attributes, like assertiveness, ambition, and independence.

According to Biller, "Women who possess both positive feminine and positive masculine characteristics and secure sex role orientations are most able to actualize their potential. Women who have pride in their femininity and are independent and assertive as well as nurturant and sensitive are likely to achieve interpersonal and creative fulfillment."

How can you encourage this in your daughter? In general, girls don't emulate their fathers as much as boys do. But studies have shown that authoritative fathers who respect and value their daughters while they motivate and even expect them to develop areas of competency outside "traditional" sex roles (such as woodworking, astronomy, or competitive team sports) influence their daughters to be successful in their relationships with men as well as in their careers.

Fathers teach sex roles to their daughters by responding to them as "interested" males. When you sit down and talk with your daughter (from toddlerhood onward) about her interests, problems, achievements, and social life while sharing your own concerns, you show her that she's important to you and that her opinions count. Because you are open and approachable, she applies this experience to other males in her life. As she grows older, she finds men less mysterious and therefore interacts with them naturally, with less temerity, and as an equal. (See Chapter 8 for a further discussion of fathers' role in their children's developing sexuality, intimacy, and the learning of sexual attitudes.)

6

How to Father Authoritatively: Providing Discipline With Love

As you've seen, the authoritative father is most effective in helping his children to develop. Providing discipline with love is the key to authoritative fathering.

Discipline is a complex issue. Many men are filled with insecurity and doubts about their role as disciplinarians. Carl's struggle is typical. "I just can't seem to get it right," he complained. "Either I'm overbearing and enraged, or I slink away and let my wife handle it. No matter what I do, I feel like the bad guy."

"Yeah," echoed Paul. "As hard as I try, I find I don't have the patience for it. When my daughter starts to whine, I want to shake her to make her stop. Or else I give her what she's nagging for—just to get her to shut up."

"I think I have it worse," said Gary. "My wife won't lift a finger against the kids when they misbehave. She just gathers up all their mischief and dumps it on my lap the minute I walk in the door. It reminds me of that old TV series, "Wait Till Your Father Gets Home." I tell her I don't deserve to be the policeman all the time. But in her family, her dad did all the disciplining, so she claims that's the right way for us to handle it. To me it feels like she's copping out. I especially hate being put in the position of disciplinarian because I see my kids so little and I end up being angry with them when I do. Is that any way to be a father?"

Confusions About Discipline and Control

Why do so many men have difficulty with discipline? To begin with, although not the sole disciplinarians (mothers teach by example and have more contact with kids than dads may), men historically have been regarded as the rule enforcers in the family. Traditionally, it has been the father's job to instill values, morals, responsibility, independence, and self-reliance in children—a sometimes unenviable task. The childhood experience of Gary's wife is not so far from the traditional norm, even if her demands made Gary uncomfortable.

Second, although we may not want to be like our fathers, we often unconsciously perpetuate our parents' discipline approach because we have no other model. Or, as in Carl's situation, not wanting to be violent, we withdraw, leaving the entire responsibility of discipline to our wives.

Third, men's difficulties with discipline issues often boil down to a question of control. We may feel out of control in our lives because of work-related stress, financial pressures, marital conflicts, or illness. Anxiety and fear grow proportionately. In order to gain some mastery over our lives, our need to create order may spill over into our interactions with our families. At our workplace, for example, we have specific assignments required of us. Once accomplished, we move on to the next tasks. Frequently, our work entails both giving and receiving orders along a certain chain of command. Even if we are juggling twenty projects at once, we can have an underlying sense of the organization.

In the world of families and relationships, however, the roles and rules are not so clear-cut. Responsibilities shift from moment to moment. And kids can't be pigeonholed as easily as merchandise that needs cataloging, legal cases that need arguing, or carburetors that need rebuilding. People—and kids in particular—are just too unpredictable, and that sometimes makes us feel as if they are flying out of our grasp.

One of the ways that we men deal with our feelings of loss of control is to use authoritarian discipline. We want our kids to "shape up" and "get in line." We may become demanding, controlling, and inflexible. Yet this approach causes many men internal conflict and pain recalled from childhood trauma of the same sort. One father, for example, described extreme anxiety when the family was to leave any public place. His own father would say, "Okay, we're leaving now!" and anyone not ready was literally left behind.

Because of the psychological price they felt they had to pay, some sons of controlling, authoritarian fathers go the other way, wanting their interactions with their children to be marked by kindness and love. Yet sometimes this desire to have a loving relationship with their kids gets in the way of establishing appropriate limits with their children, resulting in paternal overpermissiveness.

Review your father's discipline style. Was he a bully? Did he ridicule and criticize you? How did you feel when he behaved that way? Clearly, you do not want to repeat what was so painfully done to you. Remembering how you felt helps you to empathize with your kids, thereby lessening your inclination to reenact your upbringing.

Realize that change is possible. You don't have to repeat your father's approach. Once you become aware of the source of your behavior, it is much easier to get a grip on it and modify it.

A New Understanding: Disciplining With Love

Authoritative fathering entails a new understanding of discipline. Despite how your father may have acted, discipline is not simply the controlling of "bad" behavior. Think of it, rather, as another form of love—no different from physical affection—and as a tool to teach your children about human relations, trust, compassion, and honesty. Discipline is a long-term way of relating to your kids that creates safe parameters, rather than a last-minute, "I-can't-take-any-more-of-this/you'd-better-behave-or-else" angry response to misbehavior.

Children need established rules to push against in order to define themselves. When you give in to your children's unreasonable demands, they may come to lack a firm foundation upon which to base their future decisions—when the sands shift constantly, it's difficult to maintain one's footing. Just as we do, children like the world to be predictable. When it's not, they become anxious and increasingly demanding, constantly testing the rules.

Authoritative discipline helps your kids feel contained

and safe. They know who you are, where they stand, and that you care. You won't let them watch TV past their bedtime; they can't ride their bikes after dusk; you stick by the established curfew; you won't allow them or their teenage friends to bring liquor into the house. Even though they may complain about it, your children realize that your taking a stand when you feel they are making a mistake demonstrates your commitment to protect and guide them.

Your youngsters' sense of responsibility actually grows when you discipline authoritatively, because you help them contain their impulses and become accountable for their behavior. They learn quickly that actions have consequences. At the same time, the love you express creates a feeling of trust, caring, warmth, and mutual respect in the family and gives your children a sense of self-respect and confidence. It is an interaction that is immediate and personal and that has a tremendous impact on your children's ability to deal with the world.

Why Authoritative Discipline Is Important

1. *Authoritative discipline gives children a feeling of safety and structure.* Without appropriate limits, your kids control you rather than the other way around. Children who have no limits escalate their demands and unseemly behavior. They are asking in their own way for you to contain and comfort them. They feel anxious when you don't take charge because they fear you will also abdicate your responsibility when it comes to protecting them.

2. *Undisciplined children find it hard to get along with others as they grow to maturity.* Kids who have not been appropriately disciplined have a tough time as teenagers and adults because they may have developed inappropriate social skills. A child, for example, whose manipulations, nagging, and whining are acceded to at home has no limits and does not take responsibility for her actions. Instead, she learns to make excuses for her behavior. This child may not listen to her teachers or friends. When denied a request, she simply amplifies her demands. Others perceive such youngsters as aggressive and disruptive. Children don't like to be around playmates who always get their own way and who won't share.

3. *Children of permissive parents often act more outrageously as a way of forcing adults to set limits.* Some fathers fear that if they set limits, they are squelching their children's independence. Yet since children need limits in order to feel secure, they will do whatever they can to get parents to provide some. That may mean escalating negative behavior, such as kicking the dog, refusing to go to school, or bopping a baby brother on the head with a Teenage Mutant Ninja Turtle. In adolescence, acting out can take the form of sexual promiscuity and drug or alcohol abuse.

4. *Authoritarian discipline does more harm than good.* It diminishes a child's self-esteem. Authoritarian fathers won't listen to their kids because they're more interested in having them follow the rules than exploring the issues. Consequently, youngsters can't use interactions with their dads to learn from their mistakes, change, and grow. Rather, they withdraw, feeling that their ideas and concerns won't be acknowledged. This may lead to lying

to cover up mistakes for fear of further verbal and physical punishment. Lying intensifies the loss of self-esteem, since the child knows she has both committed an infraction and been dishonest about it.

Take, for example, the third-grader who fails spelling tests but avoids reporting it for fear of her authoritarian father's wrath. Rather, she throws the tests away. Come Open School Night, the father may discover the string of failures, which leads to a downward spiral of disparagement and punishment rather than an investigation of what went wrong, why the material seems so difficult, and how the father can help. Instead, the child may be showered with such criticisms as "You're lazy," "You don't study enough," "You're a liar," "You'll never amount to anything." The authoritarian father takes his daughter's failures personally, as if they're a reflection of his parenting abilities rather than a normal part of growth.

Understandably, children of authoritarian fathers feel powerless and angry, and may redirect these negative feelings into hostile and provocative behavior toward other children. They may pick fights with classmates, tease siblings to tears, break family heirlooms, play roughly with favorite toys, or hurt pets and other small animals.

The Mechanics of Authoritative Discipline

Authoritative discipline consists of four straightforward steps:

* Set the limits.
* Create an appropriate consequence.
* Follow through consistently.
* Make the system involve choice.

These four elements must all exist or the whole system falls apart. Think of it as you would your car: the drive train, steering mechanism, engine, transmission, and fuel injection system must all work together, or the car breaks down.

Let's see how these four elements of discipline work. Using one situation, we'll follow it through the four-step sequence for the sake of clarity. Suppose that an ongoing conflict in your home revolves around Billy cleaning up his room. Here's the scenario:

You want Billy to put away all of his junk before he goes to bed each evening. His bedtime is supposed to be 8 P.M., but he is usually so engrossed in his Nintendo game that he won't respond until you raise the roof, usually at about 8:15. By then, the room is still a mess, it's already late, and you're fuming. You feel trapped because you want him to get a full night's sleep, but his room just seems to get worse and worse. And he is triumphant, having managed to wriggle out of your expectations one more night. Here's what to do:

1. *Set the limits.* Often limit setting is easy for men. We are used to meeting deadlines and thinking of problems in terms of concrete actions. In the case of Billy's room, set aside some quiet time, say, after dinner or on a weekend, when you can both air your feelings about the problem without anger or hostility. Then voice your expectation that he will clean up his room each night before turning in. You need not be threatening or indignant. Just be firm. You're simply stating the limit.

2. *Create an appropriate consequence.* Men tend to have more difficulty with this step. Often, seeking a quick solution to a thorny problem, dads adopt consequences that are either meaningless ("Go to your room!") or overly harsh ("You're grounded for a month!") as a way just to get the job done.

   An appropriate consequence should take the form of an if-then statement: "If your room isn't cleaned up by eight o'clock tomorrow evening (and every night after that), then . . ." You may choose any number of consequences that fit the "crime." For example:

   • " . . . you won't be able to play Nintendo tomorrow."
   • " . . . I will put away (or throw away) any toys that are left on the floor and you won't have them to play with anymore." (We did this only once with our kids—that's all it took.)
   • " . . . I won't buy you the new Slime Oozer you've been asking for."

   Sometimes my wife and I asked our daughters about what they thought an appropriate consequence would be.

Often their suggestions were more severe than what we would have proposed. And they were more apt to abide by the consequence if they had a hand in creating it. Make sure, though, that the consequence is in some way related to the situation. Depriving Billy of dessert, for example, may work if he pilfers the cookie jar before dinner, but it doesn't seem appropriate for a messy room. Spanking or physical punishment is never appropriate.

Never make idle threats, such as "You'd better clean up, or else," or "If you don't clean up by eight o'clock, I'll never buy you another toy." At first, these may frighten your child, but once she realizes that you have no intention of following through, she'll just learn to ignore what you say. You'll find yourself endlessly nagging—the hallmark of a permissive father.

By the way, children can tell the difference between punishment and consequences. Punishments are usually inflicted on your children in the heat of anger. Consequences, on the other hand, are a natural, logical outgrowth of your children's actions. Kids resent and rebel at punishment but respond to consequences.

3. *Follow through consistently.* Consistency isn't easy, but it's crucial. To maintain consistency, the consequence you have chosen must fall into the range of what you are capable of doing. If, for example, you have promised Billy that he won't be able to play with his Nintendo the following evening, but then you're out at a business meeting on the designated night and forget to tell the babysitter, Billy may feel free to do as he pleases. The consequence will have no meaning to him. Indeed, he may ignore your limits all the more.

If you're reluctant to throw away your child's toys

(after all, it's your hard-earned money that's being dumped into the garbage), then don't impose that consequence. In order for this system to work, you must be willing to follow through each and every time that Billy breaks the rules or else have a plan to follow in case you're not personally available to oversee the consequence. Furthermore, if you haven't followed through, it's important to say to your kids, "I made a mistake. I'll make sure to enforce the consequence tomorrow night."

When you carry out consequences only sporadically, you are actually reinforcing negative behavior. Which one is it, your child wonders. Room cleanup or no cleanup? Nintendo or no Nintendo? Since he can't count on the rules being enforced, he becomes confused.

Behavioral scientists performing experiments with pigeons showed that on-again, off-again limits and consequences are worse than none at all. The pigeons in these experiments were placed in cages with levers. The birds learned that after every ten pecks on the lever, they would be rewarded with a pellet of food. They received consistent and predictable reinforcement for their pecking behavior.

Then the scientists changed the experiment. Altering the levers, the machines now delivered food pellets randomly. Sometimes the pellets popped out after the first peck. Sometimes it took twenty pecks for the pigeon to get the reward. In scientific terms this is called an *intermittent reinforcement schedule*. Rather than reduce the pigeon's pecking, it increased the rate dramatically.

What does this mean to you, Billy, and the messy room? You'll teach your child to test the limits all the more if you're inconsistent in your response. The behavior you're wanting to eliminate (leaving a messy room) or change will increase or worsen. You must choose a consequence that you can live with and then apply it each and every time that Billy does not stick to the limits you've established. When you're consistent in your follow-through, he will learn that *you mean what you say and you say what you mean!*

4. *Make the system involve choice.* This is fairly easy. You can state the consequence as a choice: "Either you clean up your room by eight o'clock or there will be no Nintendo tomorrow. It's up to you. I trust you to make the right decision." Because the child chooses, he begins to learn how to take responsibility for his own actions. Of course, the situation may leave him feeling between a rock and a hard place, but he still has some control. He can actually choose to clean up his room.

If Billy sticks to the limits you've established, make sure to praise him to the skies. You can say: "I see you've chosen to clean up your room. That's just wonderful. You've done a great job. I'm really proud of you. And tomorrow, you get to play Nintendo until cleanup time." You'll be using *positive reinforcement,* which is the most effective way of changing a child's behavior. He'll want to repeat the same behavior the next evening.

If, on the other hand, Billy has continued his game until 8:10, testing your limits (as he's surely apt to do), you can *calmly* say, "I see you've chosen not to play Nintendo tomorrow. That's too bad. Well, maybe tomorrow night, if you clean up on time, you'll choose to get your game back."

The variations on this simple formula are endless. For example, if Johnny pokes Fido, you can say:

"It's not okay to hurt a dog. If you poke Fido, I will take him away for ten minutes. It's up to you."

Johnny may test the limit by poking the dog again.

You should respond, "By your actions, you have chosen to have me take Fido away. I will put him downstairs for ten minutes."

When you follow through, your children may throw tantrums to voice their displeasure and frustration, gain your attention, and get the plaything back. What do you do then? Why not try a time-out? (You'll find further advice for calming a tantrum in the next chapter.)

Time-Outs Are Helpful in Authoritative Fathering

Men understand time-outs as they're used in sports. In basketball, for instance, the coach may call for a time-out when the team has fallen behind. The players need a moment to reevaluate their strategy, and the coach has the opportunity to advise them about weaknesses in their or their opponents' play.

Sometimes it's helpful to give yourself the same sort of breather to regroup and rethink after your kids have caused havoc. In taking a few minutes to think the issues through, you avoid jumping impulsively into an overly permissive or excessively punitive consequence.

Depending on your child's age, a time-out can also be an appropriate consequence in itself. It's especially useful if your kids are squabbling. In that case, your statement to them would be: "If you girls can't play without fighting over your Barbies, then I'll have to separate you for ten minutes. It's up to you."

If they can't work out their differences with words and again resort to hitting each other, you can say, "I see you weren't able to handle playing for now. You need a time-out. Melissa, sit in the den. Janey, go to the living room. You'll each have to sit there for ten minutes. While you're having your time-out, I want each of you to think about how *you* contributed to this problem. I'll be in to talk to you about it in ten minutes." Use the time to formulate your own authoritative four-step approach.

A few important points to remember about time-outs:

1. *Use a matter-of-fact voice.* If your child is engaging in mischief to get your attention, anger on your part will convey to him that he has been successful. (Angry attention is better than no attention at all!) Just state the facts: Here's what you've done; this is the consequence that you've chosen.

2. *Use verbal and nonverbal communication.* If your child is actually hitting a playmate, say "Stop!" and separate them.

3. *Make sure you send your child to a neutral environment.* Banishing your five-year-old to his room is about as effective as sending him to Disneyland. There are lots of interesting activities to engage his attention there. You'd want him to take his time-out in a place that's dull and unstimulating. A stool in the kitchen, for example, is ideal.

4. *Monitor your child's behavior during the time-out.* If the consequence was imposed because of a tantrum, make

sure your son has calmed down before he is allowed to join the family again. (Obviously, if he's still carrying on, you will reinforce the tantrum by excusing him while it's still in progress.) This is a good time to talk about why the time-out was imposed, your child's contributions to the problem, and what changes would prevent time-outs in the future.

5. *Set an appropriate length of time.* For toddlers, the general rule of thumb is that the number of minutes of the time-out should equal the child's age. Increase the time accordingly as your child grows, but set a limit in advance unless you're dealing with a tantrum.

Positive Reinforcement: The Key to Authoritative Fathering

An article in the *New York Times* recently noted that Lawrence J. Pijeaux, Jr., the principal of the L. B. Landry Magnet School, a campus that draws its students from the most impoverished section of New Orleans, won an American Heroes in Education award from *Reader's Digest* for his extraordinary achievements.

When Pijeaux became principal of the seventh-through-twelfth-grade school in 1982, it had a dropout rate of 30 percent. Only 5 percent of the students went on to college, and test scores were the lowest in the district. Through his efforts, Pijeaux was able to cut the dropout rate in half to 15 percent, and 30 percent of the students are accepted at colleges. In addition, test scores now rank in the top third of the district.

How was Pijeaux able to achieve this remarkable turn-around? Simple. He used praise. He helped build his students' self-esteem. According to the article, "Academic and athletic achievers received T-shirts, buttons and certificates; newsletters and bulletins trumpeted their names through the school and the community. 'It sounds very simplistic,' [Pijeaux] said, 'but it's real.' "

When you focus only on your children's inadequacies—what they do wrong—they eventually get the message that they can never do anything right. Your kids yearn for your approval. If you don't give it to them, they'll try to get your attention in any way they can, even if it means doing something that you disapprove of.

Praise or positive reinforcement helps to change your children's behavior. If you extoll the virtues of your youngster's leaf-raking job (even if she hasn't picked up every last oak leaf), then she'll feel motivated to try harder the next time. If, on the other hand, you only point out what she missed, she'll feel defeated. "Why should I try?" she may think. "Daddy never likes what I do anyway."

You can alter behavior by combining the limit setting/ consistent consequence program with positive reinforcement. The first part helps eliminate negative behavior, while the second part supports the change.

When using praise, however, it's important for you to learn to accept *successive approximations.* Successive approximations means that your kids may not get the whole task right the first, second, or even third time around. But you should still praise their attempts. Gradually, as they master the behavior you are requesting, you can become more exacting. For example, in the case of pet responsibilities, you can say, "Jason, I love the way you fed Prince today. You washed his bowl and gave him the right amount of food. Tomorrow, let's see if you can put the sack of dog food away, too."

To be most effective, be generous with your positive statements. Praise is a powerful self-esteem builder and teaching tool. When you use positive reinforcement, you become the antithesis of the critical, authoritarian father.

Getting Down to Your Child's Level

When providing discipline, it's important for you to get down to your child's level physically. In my workshop, I ask fathers to sit on the floor while I perch on a chair and lecture to them. The men suddenly experience the vulnerability of a three-year-old. They appreciate how difficult it is to pay attention from that vantage point—they must crane their necks just to see my face. For a child, a big, loud man can be frightening, even if he's Daddy.

When you want to communicate, get to a level where eye contact is easy. You can both be sitting, or you can kneel on the floor. And talk in a normal tone of voice. You will perceive your child as being less defensive, and she'll be less likely to ignore you or to rebel. By bringing yourself to her level, you are demonstrating that you respect her feelings and personhood.

In addition to getting down to your child's level physically, it's important to reach her emotionally. You do that by really listening to her explanation of what went wrong. The communication techniques called *active listening, mirroring,* and *eye contact* are most helpful in this regard.

During active listening, you repeat back to your child what you just heard her say, without value judgments. Active listening helps to ensure that you have understood your child's point of view. It gives you the opportunity to hear her feelings without necessarily doing anything about them, and it reassures her that her concerns have registered. Active listening can also be practiced in reverse: your child can repeat your point of view back to you.

Mirroring is a variation of active listening in which you reflect your child's emotions back to her, thereby letting her know that you understand her frustration or pain even though you may not agree with her chosen course of action. You can say, for example, "I know you really feel angry about your baby sister and wish you still had me all to yourself, but it's not okay for you to hit her." Then follow up with a consequence and a choice as outlined above. Mirroring helps to validate your child's feelings by showing her that you care about them.

Eye contact also helps make an emotional connection. You express your feelings—especially love—through your eyes. When you make eye contact with your youngster, you're letting him know that what he has to say is important.

Family Meetings

Family meetings are a time set aside, either routinely, like every week, or when you, your wife, or even your kids feel something in the family is amiss. You may want to hold routine meetings even without a troublesome problem because they regularize communications and help you monitor the state of the family. Crises will be lessened if meetings occur frequently, since you'll be continually defusing problems before they can stockpile and reach a critical mass.

Parents usually initiate meetings, though children can, too. You'll need to watch time concerns. Allow ten or twenty minutes, depending on your children's ages and attention spans. As your youngsters mature, they can share in the responsibility for choosing the issues to discuss or the format of the meeting. It's best to deal with a single subject, such as jealousy over the new baby or how to help your daughter get to sleep. Depending on the situation, you may take a vote, as to which movie you're all going to see or where (within the parameters you've established) you'll take your summer vacation. For other issues such as curfews, TV time, or a thirty-girl Halloween slumber party, ultimately you may have the final authority. But at least your kids will have had the opportunity to air their needs and feel listened to and validated.

During these meetings, all of the traditional rules are suspended. Each person gets equal time to have his or her say. Each feels acknowledged. This helps your child to gain a sense of his own importance and encourages his feeling of responsibility for his own acts. It also helps you to understand your child's concerns in a caring, nonthreatening environment. Make sure you are not interrupted by phone calls or other distractions.

You may ask Seth, for example, to help you understand why he has been acting so angrily lately. It's not like him to throw his favorite toy against the wall with such vehemence. This gentle confrontation will help him put his feelings into words rather than act them out. And he may discover that his words and feelings have an impact on you. He may say, for example, that you have been picking on him lately.

If this causes you to reassess your own behavior, he'll come to see that he has some power in the family.

Although you may not always resolve all of your problems during your family meetings (it's quite all right to leave issues unresolved and open to further discussion), often just clearing the air helps to reduce frustration and anger. Family meetings also create closeness and understanding. In our family we usually end our meetings with a hugging session—it's a great way to express love.

The Dangers of Labeling

One of the cardinal rules of authoritative discipline is never to label your kids or call them names; always separate the *act* from the *person*. Make "I" statements rather than "you" statements. For instance, if your daughter spills her milk all over her clothes say, "I don't like it when you're not careful," instead of, "God, you're so clumsy," "You're a *bad* girl for spilling your milk," or "What's wrong with you?" When you stick to "I" statements, your feelings about your child have not been brought into question. She'll understand that you still find her lovable; you just don't like what she did.

When you use such expressions as "bad," "naughty," "lazy," "stupid," or "sloppy," your child feels worthless, rejected, and fearful of losing your love. He may despair of ever changing your opinion of him. In fact, these kinds of words can create *self-fulfilling prophecies*. Your child may reason, "Well, if Daddy thinks I'm bad, then I must really be bad. So I might as well act that way."

Conversely, it's not a good idea to call your daughter a

"good girl" when you praise her. If she's good today, she may be bad tomorrow. Instead, heap on specific praise about her actions. "Wow!" you could say. "You did a fabulous job on that report. You must be happy with yourself. I'm really proud of you."

Also, watch words like "always" and "never." When you say, "You *always* get into trouble when we go out," or "You *never* listen," you are reinforcing your child's negative view of himself. He feels as if his misdeeds are chiseled in stone and that he can never redeem himself. Instead, make specific "I" statements, such as, "I don't like it when you keep throwing the spoon on the floor," or "I feel frustrated and angry when I ask you to walk the dog and you don't."

Spanking

Spanking is a difficult topic for most fathers. When we were children, child abuse was not the social issue it is now. No milk cartons carried abuse hot line numbers in the 1950s or '60s. I don't think I'd be too far off to say that many of us were spanked as a matter of course, so we may find it creeping into our arsenal of disciplinary weapons.

Despite the cultural shift away from corporal punishment, if your child suddenly darts into traffic or otherwise endangers herself, your reflex may be to give her a swift whack on the bottom just to make sure she remembers the lesson. But for most behavior problems, spanking is not only damaging, it is also an ineffectual method of disciplining your children. And hitting with objects like shoes, belts, or sticks not only inflicts great bodily harm, it also creates emotional scars and therefore is abusive. Any such practice is subject to investigation by protective services or the police.

Some fathers feel that spanking is the only way to get their out-of-control children to toe the line. In fact, these men are acting out of their own frustration and need for control. Spanking may quiet the disobedient child for a short time and therefore can be reinforcing to a father's ego. But in the long run, the spanked child will be angered and will act out all the more to seek revenge. This, of course, can prompt further beatings, which may escalate into truly abusive situations.

Sometimes children who have been spanked become fearful in anticipation of being spanked again. Their anxiety makes them restless and may cause them to misbehave once more. This creates a vicious cycle and can result in a frightened and nervous child. In addition, hitting teaches your child that physical violence is an acceptable way to vent frustration, anger, or disappointment. He never learns to use his words to work out problems effectively.

The whole system may break down when the child reaches adolescence. In extreme cases, the father may feel that his teenage daughter is too big to be spanked or he may fear that his son will hit back. Often parents throw up their hands and relinquish disciplinary responsibilities to school authorities or the police at this point, saying, "He's impossible. There's just nothing we can do."

Children won't outgrow the approach outlined in this chapter: set limits, create reasonable consequences, follow through consistently, and include choice. With consistent and appropriate follow-through the system works well (even into adolescence), kids do learn to control their impulses, and parents listen to and respect their children.

In the case of a child running into the street, since the natural consequence is terribly dangerous, you will need to create your own effective and enforceable consequence. For example, you may tell Ricky that if he runs into the street again, he'll be allowed to play only in the backyard for the next week, after which you'll give him a chance to show you how well he can control his behavior. But remember to be firm. Discipline breaks down when parents are unwilling to follow through on a consequence that they have set. In this case, the results could be tragic.

Power Struggles

Power struggles occur when you make an unconditional demand, such as "Do it because I say so!" or "You're only a kid. I'm your father and I know what's best for you!" Children become defensive in the face of authoritarian statements that don't respect their inner reality. Resentful, they may reply defiantly, which in turn feeds your anger. You may become even more restrictive ("If that's the way you're going to be, you can't go to Disneyland next week"), and the original issue you were arguing about gets lost in the escalating battle, not to mention that trip to Disneyland.

Gary was constantly getting into power struggles with his five-year-old daughter Cindy. Here's how he described it: "When I tell her, 'Finish your dinner,' or 'Go to bed,' she puts her little hands on her hips and says in that snide little voice of hers, 'No! I don't have to. And you can't make me!'

"This makes me so angry, I just want to scream. I feel like saying to her, 'Oh yeah? Who says I can't? I'll show you. You sit there and eat your dinner or I'll feed it to you like a baby.' "

If your child repeatedly defies your authority or oversteps the limits you've established, you may get into power struggles like Gary and Cindy's. Unfortunately, everyone loses. Even if you win, it's a hollow victory, for sooner or later you can be sure that your child will find a way to get even.

Power struggles are particularly difficult for men to handle. When dads experience their children as acting defiantly (even when the kids may simply be expressing their own emotions and frustration), they experience it as a lack of respect. Their identities and sense of authority and control are put into question and perhaps even undermined. This is especially painful if one's own father was authoritarian and exerted complete control over the family.

If you find yourself getting into power struggles, it might be advisable for you to stop for a moment and listen to the timbre of your communications. Are you taking your child's challenge as a personal affront to your role as parent? Do you feel offended if your child asserts his or her individuality by denying your request? If your ego gets caught up in the give and take, your child may be apt to resist the pressure he or she feels.

No one likes to be ordered around by a bully. In his fantasized conversation with his daughter, Gary was certainly bullying her or putting her at risk. It might have been better for Gary to say, "What I want is not so important. This is really your problem. You'll have to decide for yourself." After an agreed-upon length of time, he can take away her dinner, saying, "I guess you're not interested in eating now. When you're ready and hungry, I'm sure you'll eat." He then should make sure she doesn't snack until the next meal.

Wait Till Your Father Gets Home

What most fathers least want to hear when they get home from work is a litany of the children's misdeeds. Indeed, family conflicts occur most often during that first hour, because each family member has his or her own agenda. Father, off from work, wants to relax and unwind. But his wife—especially if she is a homemaker—sees his presence as the arrival of fresh troops. Finally, someone else to take over! For the children, it's a new person with renewed energy. They want attention and become more demanding.

If Mom works, too, the first hour home can be even more taxing. She wants to make contact with you and the kids, go over the mail, and perhaps even organize dinner. Yet she's also tired. Everyone is needy and everyone is entitled to support at this time. In fact, some couples get into competitive "war stories" at this point, over whose day was the worst.

If these problems are issues for you, a family meeting would help to bring everyone's feelings out into the open. There are several approaches that your family could take to help resolve this conflict.

1. *Take a few minutes to yourself before interacting with your family.* In our household, when Sue was teaching, she came home from work long before I did. She had a few hours with the kids before I arrived. So we resolved that I not be disturbed for twenty minutes after I walked in the door. That meant I greeted everyone and went into my room for a nap. Then, rested, I put in some time with them and gave Sue a break.

   Other families have devised different strategies. One

dad parked down the block and played a relaxation tape in his car before braving the home front. Another sat in the driveway for ten minutes. Meditations, relaxation tapes, classical music can all be used.

2. *Play with the children for five minutes and then take a nap.* If your kids are not old enough to tolerate the frustration of your absence right away, give them a short time now and promise more to come later when you're feeling better.

3. *Use music as a timing device.* You can say, "When this tape is over, I'll come out and play with you." This helps your younger children gauge and adjust to the separation. A timer may work, too.

4. *Take a few minutes with your wife just to ventilate.* This is especially helpful if you're both working. You can each get five minutes to complain about your day. Neither of you has to feel obligated to do anything about the other's stress. Then you can settle into the evening more peacefully.

In group member Gary's family, the homecoming issue was compounded by his wife's inability or unwillingness to discipline the children during the day. When couples are experiencing such a great and rigid disparity in expectations, it's a sure sign that family counseling is needed to help forge a compromise that both husband and wife can live with.

Discipline Problems or Your Unrealistic Expectations?

At one time or another, all parents see their children as extensions of themselves. As such, we may forget that little Jake is only four years old and operates under a different set of rules than we do. Consequently, sometimes discipline problems are not discipline problems at all—they are *agenda* problems. In *How to Stop the Battle with Your Child,* psychologist Don Fleming points out that "quarreling between the parent and a seemingly difficult child may simply be due to a misunderstanding between agendas."

For example, while you're at your local pizzeria waiting for your mushrooms, pepperoni, and sausage delight to finish baking, you may be content to stare at the walls, pick at your salad, and make small talk with your wife. But Jake, at four years old, has too much curiosity and energy to simply sit still for twenty minutes. He slides off his chair and explores the pedestal under the table and the sawdust on the floor. He stands in the booth and watches your neighbors enjoy their dinner. He makes three trips to the bathroom to wash his hands and splash water on the walls. His restlessness may bring out the authoritarian father in you, tempting you to shout, "Sit down and be quiet! Now! Or else!"

Is Jake an undisciplined and unruly child? Well, not necessarily. He's doing what a four-year-old does naturally: exploring his world and learning how it works. The conflict occurs because your agenda—that he sit still and act like a little gentleman—is diametrically opposed to his. But, in truth, your expectations may be unrealistic.

Try to put yourself in his place. What would you do if you

had his boundless energy and inquiring mind? In situations like these, it's best to bring along some distraction, like a new toy or a pad of paper and a few crayons. You can mirror Jake's feelings by saying, "I know it's hard for you to sit still in this restaurant." He'll probably agree with you. Weather permitting, it may help to take short walks outside to vent some of his energy and give you all peace once the pizza arrives. Or you can discuss your expectations before you leave for a restaurant and don't make it the fanciest place in town. You'll all be better off if you can be prepared for typical four-year-old behavior.

Children's Developmental Stages From a Father's Point of View

T H E R E is an ancient Zen story about three teachers. The first views his pupils as if they were empty vessels into which he must pour information. The second sees his charges as clay for which he is the potter. He molds and sculpts them to conform to an image that he considers correct. The third treats his students as if they were plants in his garden. He realizes that each flower, tree, and shrub needs the proper but unique balance of light, water, and nutrients. He does not water a cactus as he would a rose, nor does he nurture a seedling as he would a mature tree.

As a father, you may find yourself wondering which role you should take. Are you a repository for information? Or, like the potter, do you set about molding your children's personalities? While both styles are appropriate at times, when you match activities to your child's developmental stages and personality like the third teacher, you get the most out of the little time available to you.

But, you may ask, how can I know what those stages are? I never learned anything about child psychology. My wife seems to have all the answers in that area. This feeling is quite common. As psychologist Jerrold Lee Shapiro put it in an article in *Psychology Today:*

> From the moment he knows of the pregnancy, a man is thrust into an alien world. He is encouraged, instructed and cajoled to be part of the pregnancy and birth process, something he knows little about. . . . He has no role model, since his own father almost certainly didn't do what he is expected to do.

On the whole, men have not educated themselves about the intricacies of child development. It's not that they're incapable of learning, it's just that they have rarely taken the opportunity. In growing up, they've had little exposure to child care issues and now tend to leave child development to their wives.

In fact, fathering expert Michael Lamb emphasizes that parenting skills are often acquired by "on the job" training. Since "mothers are 'on the job' more than fathers are . . . ," he explains, "mothers become more sensitive to their children, more in tune with them, more aware of each child's characteristics and needs. By virtue of their lack of experience, fathers become correspondingly less sensitive and come to feel less confidence in their parenting abilities. Fathers thus continue to defer to and cede responsibility to mothers. . . . As a result, the differences between fathers and mothers become more marked over time."

Lamb goes on to say, however, that these differences are not cast in bronze. "When circumstances thrust fathers into the primary caretaking role, or when fathers choose to redefine their parental roles and their parent-child relationships, they are perfectly capable of acquiring the necessary skills."

The purpose of this chapter is to acquaint you with the behaviors, difficulties, and feelings you're likely to encounter at various developmental stages.

Understanding your child's developmental stages gives you greater compassion and enables you to empathize with her. Empathy involves a basic attitude shift away from your own needs and wishes and toward understanding your child's. Understanding what's going on with your youngster helps you to identify and validate her feelings, which, in turn, engenders a sense of self-worth. You will be able to approach your parenting activities with more confidence and with a deeper understanding of what to expect from your youngster and from yourself.

Pregnancy

Yes, pregnancy is a stage of child development! In his book *Finding Our Fathers,* Harvard psychologist Samuel Osherson asks the question, "Do men get pregnant, too?" Yes, in an emotional way, they do. Pregnancy is a very trying time in a man's life; as for the woman, it is a major life transition. In fact, in many primitive cultures, husbands take to bed during late pregnancy as if preparing themselves for labor. They mimic their wives' pregnancy symptoms in a custom that anthropologists call *couvade.*

Our culture has developed its own set of pregnancy rituals that give fathers the experience of a vicarious pregnancy. These days men are involved in prenatal and childbirth classes. The number of fathers who take part in the birth has grown dramatically over the last two decades. According to the results of a Gallup poll, in 1973 only 27 percent of American fathers were present during delivery, while in 1983, 79 percent of men participated. Dr. Susan Ludington, a professor of maternity-child health at the University of California, Los Angeles, finds that those figures still hold today. "From my clinical experience attending births at eight Los Angeles hospitals," she explained in an interview, "no less than 80 percent of fathers participate in their babies' births."

This is great news. Several studies have shown that men who have taken childbirth classes feel a stronger attachment to their kids after delivery. They touch and hold the infant more frequently, are more willing to change diapers, and in general show more warmth and empathy toward their kids. The evidence is strong that the more you are involved in your wife's pregnancy, the more physically and emotionally involved you will be with your kids eight to ten years down the road.

One investigation by Dr. H. Nickel at the University of Dusseldorf, Germany, reported that this involvement has a positive effect on the infants, as well. According to Nickel, the nine-month-old babies with "prepared" fathers "showed a higher degree of responsiveness and uttered more positive vocalizations. Further, a developmental screening revealed an advantage in some aspects of social behavior."

COMMUNICATING WITH THE FETUS

But what about during the pregnancy itself? Can fathers-to-be have some impact on their children before their birth? The surprising and exciting news is that during the last two months of gestation, many of the fetus's sensory organs are already formed and functioning. And, yes, implausible as it may seem, you may be able to influence the parent-child bond even before your baby enters the world!

Research conducted among expectant fathers shows that men begin to fantasize about their babies after the pregnancy becomes detectable in some way—either they feel the fetus's movements or they observe the fetus during an ultrasound exam. Our visions of prenatal life are gentle and romantic. We often think of the baby as floating in a quiet, warm, peaceful space. Actually, nothing could be further from the truth.

During the last two months of pregnancy, the fetus hears the mother's voice, heartbeat, and digestive sounds, and even external noises like landing airplanes, music, and bells. It exercises its limbs by pushing against the uterine walls. It sucks its thumb, swallows, and makes facial expressions that resemble crying. This stimulation helps the nervous system develop. Indeed, by the time the fetus is twenty-seven weeks old, scientists have found that it responds to movement, touch, and light. By thirty-six weeks, the fetal ear is open and fully functional.

All this means that you may be able to communicate with your fetus before birth. You may even wish to teach your developing fetus in a very gentle and loving way to recognize your voice. At birth, he may recognize the familiar sound and turn toward you.

In *How to Have a Smarter Baby,* Dr. Susan Ludington and Susan Golant suggest talking to the fetus and even making a tape of your and your wife's voices to enhance closeness and early bonding. You can call the baby by name or use a pet name (if you don't know your child's sex), repeating it often. You can also play some soothing classical music. Mozart, Brahms, or Bach is best. It need not be loud for your fetus to appreciate it.

EMOTIONAL STRESSES DURING YOUR WIFE'S PREGNANCY

While it's easy to get caught up in the excitement of this special time, you should watch out for some patches of emotional quicksand along the way, especially between you and your wife. As one researcher put it, "The birth of a child transforms the pair of lovers who conceived him into *parents*"—not quite as romantic a notion. Quite naturally, your roles and your attitudes toward each other will change.

To begin with, your reaction to impending fatherhood can evoke strong memories. Depending on the quality of your relationship with your own father, you may wish to emulate him or to reject his model, and parent your child entirely differently. Your relationship with your father may change, which can feel painful or positive to you.

Many men experience a growing sense of isolation from their wives. All the attention may be focused on her and on the fetus's well-being, yet you have needs, too, and may feel left out. As Jerrold Lee Shapiro explains, "[The husband] shows no physical signs of pregnancy, but in some ways, emotionally, he's as pregnant as she is." In fact, in a study of 227 expectant and new fathers, Shapiro was able to delineate seven major fears surrounding pregnancy that at least 40 percent of his subjects experienced. The men in the study had not expressed these concerns to their wives. How many apply to you?

• *Queasiness.* Many men are anxious about the blood and guts of delivery. Despite the Lamaze training, they are afraid they'll pass out.

• *Increased responsibility.* More than 80 percent of the fathers in this study agreed with the statement made by a twenty-two-year-old man: "One day I was going along, happy-go-lucky. The next day, I was the sole support of three people."

• *Obstetrical-gynecological matters.* The inner workings of a woman's body remain a mystery to many fathers-to-be. Men fear, with some justification, that questions may not be well tolerated by the busy and impatient ob-gyn staff.

• *Uncertain paternity.* More than half the men in this survey acknowledged nagging doubts that they were really the child's father. This, according to Shapiro, may mask a deeper fear of the monumental task of creating life.

• *Loss of spouse or child.* Women once died in childbirth in great numbers. While this is no longer the case, this anxiety can mean that as your wife turns away from you to care for the baby, you may fear being excluded from her world forever. There is also the related apprehension of the child being born damaged in some way.

• *Being replaced.* When your wife focuses inward to bond with the fetus, you may feel left out. In rare cases, this provokes a very damaging late-pregnancy affair, in which a man seeks to recover a sense of being "important."

• *Life and death.* As you suddenly feel responsible for the new child, you may begin to take fewer risks. As one man put it, "I was now important to this little thing, and I couldn't die because he needed me."

In addition, the sight of your wife's pregnant body summons new emotions. Some men lose their sexual desire for their wives at this time. They may find her distended shape unattractive, or they may become afraid of hurting the fetus. Some even regard the fetus as an intruding third party. Your wife's pregnancy may also reawaken your powerful but long-suppressed desire to be nurtured and mothered.

Some of these problems may seem ridiculous; others may touch you. The best way to deal with your feelings and fears is to acknowledge them first to yourself and then to your spouse. Sharing your concerns with your wife does not burden her (as you may fear). Rather, you increase intimacy and strengthen your relationship.

The First Year of Life

George voiced a common fear among new fathers. "I'm afraid to hold Todd," he explained. "What if I drop him? What if I squeeze him too hard? I'm worried that I'll hurt him in some way." George was suffering from what I call the Lalique glass syndrome. He was afraid of doing damage because he perceived his son as being ultra-fragile. But in a larger sense, George was afraid that he was inadequate to the task of being a parent, that he lacked the proper skills to care for his son.

Rick complained of feeling awkward when handling his newborn. A successful contractor by day, he was frustrated and irritated, seeing himself as but an "all-thumbs" father by night. He began withdrawing from Adam and leaving much of the diaper changing, bathing, and dressing to his wife, Karen. In fact, he was even starting to feel excluded and jealous of the "good time" they were having together.

Edward had a hard time relating to an infant who did nothing but "eat, poop, cry, and sleep." He thought that since Jessica couldn't yet see him or recognize his voice, there was no point in trying to develop a relationship; he'd wait until toddlerhood.

It's common for men to feel fearful and inept with their newborns. (Women do, too.) We don't have many caretaking role models. Yet fathering activities can begin at the moment of birth, even in the delivery room.

GETTING TO KNOW YOUR NEWBORN

Infants learn purely through their senses; they have not yet mastered imitation or abstract and symbolic thought. Yet the latest research in the field of child development shows that newborns have amazing abilities. Your newborn

- Sees clearly within thirteen inches of her face and prefers to look at faces—especially her mother's and father's.
- Can recognize her primary caregiver's face by four days of age.
- Can follow appealing objects (especially

black-and-white geometric shapes) that are held ten to thirteen inches from her eyes.
• Distinguishes the loudness and pitch of sounds and turns her head to find sounds.
• Can differentiate between speech and nonspeech sounds by twelve hours of age.
• Recognizes your and your wife's voices within one week.
• Has a keen sense of touch and very sensitive skin.
• Can differentiate between sweet, sour, and bitter tastes and reacts accordingly.
• Distinguishes the scent of her mother's breast milk from the scent of all other mothers' milk within hours of birth.
• Can recognize the scent of your clothing and aftershave by one month of age.

Because of her already acute senses, your newborn can tell her parents apart and reacts to each of you with distinctly different behavior. This occurs as early as four weeks. And, according to fathering expert Michael Lamb, infants become attached to both parents "from the earliest age" and in some circumstances prefer their fathers. Knowing this, it's hard to justify waiting until the child is a toddler before initiating a relationship with her.

PLAYING WITH YOUR INFANT

There are many ways to relate to your infant. Try a gentle massage. Lay him down naked on your bed in a warm room and stroke his head from the forehead to the nape of the neck several times. Then continue stroking from head to toe and from the body out to the extremities. This simple massage not only feels good to him and has a calming effect, it also aids in his digestion and in the maturation of his nervous system. And it feels good to you, too.

You can play games like "Monkey see, monkey do." Mimic your baby's behavior. If he sticks out his tongue, you do the same. If he bats his eyelashes, follow his lead. In fact, if you make an interesting face—say, a look of surprise— you may find that he tries to copy you, as well, behavior called *contingency responding*. Studies have shown that infants as young as three days old can recognize and imitate facial expressions. Create a relationship any way that feels comfortable. Contingency responding shows your baby that you value his company and are trying to relate to him. It's communication.

I used to enjoy letting my infant daughters lie on my bare chest on weekend mornings when I didn't have to rush out to work. They would struggle to raise their heads to look into my eyes. This simple activity enhances bonding. It provides needed skin-to-skin contact. The eye contact is essential in expressing feelings and forming strong emotional ties. And research shows that children learn to identify their parents by the scent of their skin.

Of course, you can also talk and sing to your child. Newborns love high-pitched singsong voices; you'll notice that women naturally use this tone of voice with infants. When you talk, call your child by name and tell him how much you love him. Holding your baby in a rocking chair and singing to him as you give him a bottle and look into his eyes is a wonderful way to connect deeply. Even if your baby is napping, you can look in on him and study his fine features. You will experience feelings of warmth, love, and engrossment.

Bonding depends on contact—the more and the earlier, the better. There's no right or wrong way to go about it. Such bonding is not just the province of mothers, and the benefits are tremendous.

Most important is to have special time with your baby, even for short periods. If at all possible, take time off from work in the early weeks to be at home. You can run errands with your infant securely tucked into a baby carrier while your wife is preparing dinner. You can take over one or two bottle feedings in the evening. You can spend time alone with your infant when your wife takes a nap, goes grocery shopping, or gets a much-needed haircut on a Saturday afternoon. You and your child will get used to one another, and you'll gain confidence, as your relationship blossoms.

Problem Areas in Your Relationship With Your Infant

Along with moments of intense joy, early infancy has its moments of stress and difficulty. This is a time of adjustment for all of you, and certain issues will inevitably arise.

JEALOUSY OF THE MOTHER-CHILD BOND

Many men miss their wives' companionship once their child is born. Simple pleasures, like going out for dinner and a movie or taking a romantic weekend vacation, become complicated, if not impossible. The "friendship" aspect of the relationship seems to get lost in concerns about feeding schedules, diaper rash, and colic. For some men, the much-anticipated arrival of the child turns into the dread that their sweetheart has abandoned them for someone new—she's always too busy, tired, preoccupied, or difficult to get hold of. Sleep deprivation makes both of you cranky and vulnerable.

Sheer exhaustion is an issue. As a result of the intense need to be "good" mothers, women sometimes wear themselves out. Constantly hovering over the baby, some mothers act as if they are the only or the best person qualified to take care of the child, which can leave their spouses feeling excluded, intruded upon, or hurt. (See Chapter 2 for suggested solutions to this problem.)

Even though men may understand intellectually that their wives need to engross themselves in their children, for many, a deep sense of loneliness settles in at this time. The intensity of the mother-baby bond may also stir up long-buried feelings of sadness and loss as the new father reconnects with his own early childhood experiences. Perhaps his mother was less sensitive to his needs; perhaps he craves the bond he perceives developing between his wife and his new son—an unconditionally loving connection he himself never experienced. Jealousy is natural.

Disruption of the new parents' sex lives is common, too. Wives can be too tired or uncomfortable with the physical changes to their body. Sexual arousal causes lactating breasts to secrete milk. An infant, well attuned to the scent, can detect it even through closed doors! His call to be fed will, of course, do much to squelch your ardor, evoking even more intense feelings of jealousy and deprivation.

Yet these feelings of isolation and loneliness give you all

the more reason to bond to your child. Infants are so easy to love, they return love unconditionally. And you'll realize you're capable and competent. So get involved!

If, for instance, you envy their closeness when your wife nurses the baby, why not give the infant a bottle of expressed breast milk once or twice a day? Your wife will likely welcome the respite, and you'll have the opportunity to cradle your child in your arms. It's also possible for your wife to nurse the baby in bed as you all cuddle together.

Make an effort to utilize resources available to you. Hire a sitter or ask your in-laws to watch the baby during nap time so the two of you can slip out for an hour, even if it's just to take a walk around the local shopping mall and enjoy an ice cream cone. Bear in mind that your lives will return to normal in time. Infancy doesn't last forever!

CRYING AND SPOILING

Crying is a means for babies, especially newborns, to communicate. Infants cry for all kinds of reasons, including when:

• They feel discomfort stemming from hunger, wet diapers, gas pains and indigestion, teething, or colic.
• They're too hot or too cold.
• They're tired, bored, or frustrated.
• They're sick.

Believe it or not, you will learn to distinguish your infant's various cries. A hungry baby sounds different from one who is in pain or simply bored. Dr. Donald Turner and

Dr. Jeffrey Helms of Mitchell College in New London, Connecticut, have developed a system of cues to help parents identify the reason for their babies' cries. If your baby's cry is

• Loud and insistent and he's bending his knees, he may have colicky pain. (Flex his legs at the hips, rub his back, and try to burp him.)
• Fretful and he's passing gas or green stool, he may have indigestion. (Call your pediatrician.)
• Fretful and he's putting his fingers in his mouth and flexing and tensing his arms and legs, he may be hungry. (Feed him.) After six months of age he may be teething.
• Whiny, weak, or listless, he may be ill. (Call your pediatrician.)
• Sharp and shrill, he may be hurt. (Call your pediatrician.)

Your child will develop particular behavior patterns you'll come to recognize. In our household, crying in conjunction with ear rubbing was usually a sign of sleepiness.

Teething can be the cause not only of crying but also of excessive drooling, stomach upset and diarrhea, and irritating diaper rash. Some children who are cutting teeth even develop respiratory infections and run a mild fever. Commercial teething rings and gels are available to help alleviate your baby's suffering. But if you're really concerned or if your child is having a hard time of it, don't hesitate to consult with your pediatrician about analgesics or other strategies to help deal with this normal but difficult part of development.

It may help you to know that many babies are naturally fussier in the late afternoon and early evening, when they release tension that has built up over the day. They cry to block out any new stimulation. This, of course, usually occurs when you and your wife are trying to deal with dinner! Unfortunately, this type of crying may be difficult to quiet, and you may find yourself eating dinner with your free arm while you hold your wailing infant in your other.

Fathers with infants ask me most often if they will "spoil" their babies by responding too quickly when they cry. Tim was reluctant, for example, to answer his four-month-old's cries for fear of creating a precedent. The unequivocal answer is that it is impossible to spoil a baby by picking him up when he's crying. It's imperative to attend to him each and every time that he cries for the sake of his growing sense of security, trust, and comfort. In fact, spoiling has little to do with infants' crying, and you certainly won't spoil your children by tending to them when they are in distress. (On the other hand, toddlers and preschoolers may cry because they don't like the limits you have set. Immediately giving in to their tears in a permissive manner when they don't get their way may lead to spoiling in an older child. See toddler development below and also the discussion of limits and permissiveness in Chapter 6.) Strategies for coping with crying at bedtime and during the night are discussed on page 154.

An eight-month-old may cry because she wants you to pick her up and play with her. This is a normal part of social maturation. Like the rest of us, she wants to be with the people she loves. She enjoys your smiles and playful touch and may feel lonely and bored in the crib. Crying has successfully obtained relief from physical discomforts such as hunger, thirst, wet diapers, and coldness. Why not use it to alleviate emotional discomfort? Crying is not inappropriate in these instances. After all, this is how your child lets you know what's on her mind. But how should you respond?

First of all, take the crying seriously. Check the diaper. Try a bottle. Is there a fever? Is she teething? Does she cry in the crib but break into a broad smile when you hold her? That's a sure sign she wants to play. There's nothing wrong with that, but it's up to you to determine if it's playtime. The middle of the night, or when you've just put her down for a nap, usually doesn't qualify.

Sometimes, in fact, children become distressed and frustrated when all of their needs aren't instantly fulfilled. Then they cry angrily. It would be up to you and your wife to decide if you want to interact with your youngster at this time. Realizing that babies understand your tone of voice and what you're saying long before they can speak, your approach with your child might be, "I know you want me to pick you up now, but it's time for your nap. I'll play with you after you wake up." If you're lucky, she will fall asleep. On other occasions, however, nothing works. I don't know a single parent who hasn't paced the floors at night hugging and soothing a baby who needed to be held but who still couldn't seem to settle down.

The Terrible Twos

Toddlerhood is a time of boundless energy and excitement for your child. He is mobile, curious, and busy exploring his world while he develops a sense of identity. His motor skills develop at a rapid rate. Usually he begins walking at or near his first birthday and soon learns to run and climb. He builds towers out of wooden blocks, pounds on a toy piano, and pulls a toy along behind him. His understanding and use of language grow dramatically.

Whereas an infant learns from his senses, the toddler learns by imitating you and your wife. And so the curious toddler wants to be involved in everything that you're doing: grasping and turning the screwdriver with hot, clumsy fingers and making pies out of sand and mud; playing with the pens and important papers on your desk and wiggling the knobs on your stereo.

Your toddler also is beginning to carry on real conversations—to ask for what he wants and to let you know *loudly* what he doesn't want. In the process, he may become balky as well as bossy. As Dr. Burton L. White explains in *The First Three Years of Life,* during toddlerhood, your child first becomes aware that he is an entirely separate entity from you. He starts to use his own name, becomes possessive of his toys and clothes, and resists your rules and directions. During this "no" stage, Dr. White explains, "the child seems to be providing his [parents] with a preview of the coming attractions of adolescence."

When your toddler says no, he asserts his independence. This normal stage in his developing sense of self is called *separation and individuation.* He needs to defy authority and test limits in order to proclaim his identity. Yet as your toddler moves out into the world, these bursts of independence are punctuated with moments of clinginess in which the child seems permanently attached to a parent's leg or shirt.

A toddler understands that objects still exist when he can

no longer see them, as in such games as peekaboo (the concept of *object constancy*). Yet she still may experience intense anxiety when she has to separate from her parents. She hasn't yet learned to hold the image of her parents inside—an image that would help her feel secure when they're not present. A *transitional object,* such as a special blanket or cuddly toy, may help her feel comforted and secure. As the ego develops further, the older toddler will eventually demonstrate the *internalization* of her parents by gladly going off to nursery school (sometimes with a blanket in tow).

The toddler masters the use of his smile to beguile and manipulate those around him. A myriad of social skills include gaining adults' attention, asking them for help, expressing affection and anger, and getting the family to do what he wants.

Toddlers also begin socializing with playmates. Two-year-olds play side by side, watching one another's games. Between the ages of two and four, however, your child moves from being egocentric—where everything is I, me, mine—to learning cooperation. As he gets older, games in which toys and fantasies are shared begin to predominate.

Problems During Toddlerhood

Parents often become exhausted from chasing their toddlers around, making sure that they're not getting into anything dangerous. They're also worn out from dealing with the "no" stage, tantrums, sleep problems, and toilet training.

Much of the conflict for fathers of toddlers is between

your child's budding independence and your own need to maintain a semblance of control over his behavior. You may see your child's eating, sleeping, and toileting habits as a reflection on you personally, as if you're a "good" father only if your kid cooperates on cue. If he doesn't behave in accordance with your expectations, you feel angry.

If you find yourself embroiled in power struggles with your toddler that make you inappropriately angry, it's important to take a moment to reflect on your response. Try to separate your child's acts from your assessment of him as a person and from your own ego needs. Speak to your toddler in neutral, matter-of-fact tones—you're concerned about his health and well-being.

Don't take developmental issues personally. Bladder control, for instance, may have less to do with your child's willingness than with physiological readiness. As much as he wants to use the potty, he still is unable to connect the sensation of a full bladder with the need to seek out a toilet, or he may lack the muscle control. There's little point in yelling at him for wetting his pants. Such difficulties are part of your child's struggle to grow up.

In addition, this stage can cause conflict with your wife. As a couple, you'll need to agree on how to deal with these daily irritations in a consistent way. Support each other and present a united front. After all, kids want what they want when they want it. Your toddler will sense when you and your wife are not in agreement, and if she can play one of you against the other, she will.

If there's a lot of contention about the child's sleeping, eating, or toileting habits, they may only be the stage upon which other conflicts are playing themselves out. Excessive fighting over child rearing may indicate that the problem is less with the toddler than with the marriage. Try not to take it out on your child. A good therapist can help with counseling and communications skills.

Finally, the key to enjoying these toddler years is to not take your child's assertions of independence personally or experience them as a rejection. Pick your battles wisely— not everything is worth fighting over. It doesn't matter if she wants to smear catsup on her pancakes or to wear her parka in July. It does matter if he wants to let go of your hand in the middle of the street.

This is a wonderful age. Toddlers and preschoolers have a tremendous sense of excitement and curiosity about the world around them that can be infectious. Some men even move into a flex schedule to be with their children during these years, savoring this period of innocence.

The "No" Stage and Tantrums

When our older daughter, Cherie, entered toddlerhood, we thought that the "terrible twos" only happened in other families. After all, our baby was *perfect*. She would never carry on like those other children we saw. Boy, were we ever wrong, and we were horrified. What had happened to our lovely child?

I reassure fathers that their toddler's no's are perfectly normal. For early self-esteem, it may even be wise to let a toddler win some of the disputes she has with you. She is becoming a separate person.

Men in particular find the "no" stage difficult because they often feel the need to be in control. Children's contrariness is perceived as a threat to their authority. A toddler's no can be infuriating. Awareness of the child's underlying need to oppose your wishes, however, may help you take it less personally. It's not just your authority she's questioning, it's everyone's.

There are times, on the other hand, when your toddler's no can clash with a limit—she refuses to sit down in the shopping cart; you're off to visit Grandma on a snowy day, but she won't put on her warm tights and wool hat; she spurns your attempts to get her properly buckled into her car seat. If you persist, your child may throw a tantrum.

Tantrums are exhausting and upsetting, especially for children. But they do occur with some regularity among toddlers and preschoolers. The following step-by-step approach to curbing tantrums, which is adapted from *Disciplining Your Preschooler and Feeling Good about It*, co-authored with my wife, Susan Golant, should help you when you're faced with this problem:

1. *Separate yourself from your child.* If possible, leave the room. Eye contact with you can keep your toddler going indefinitely, or he may discern from your body language that you're emotionally invested in his behavior. Send him to his room or let him cry it out in the den while you're in the kitchen. Whatever you do, don't burst in on him after five minutes and yell at him to stop. This adds fuel to the fire!

2. *Don't try to talk sense into him.* This is not the time to reason with your youngster. The best bet is to firmly but calmly repeat: "When you're done screaming, I'll be waiting for you in the kitchen. Then you can tell me with your *words* what's bothering you. I can't talk to you when you carry on like that."

3. *Be persistent and creative.* After a few minutes of all-out pandemonium, you may feel tempted to step in. You may feel guilty or uncomfortable or perhaps angry and retaliatory. One father spanked his son every time the youngster had a tantrum, saying, "If you're going to cry, I'll give you something to cry about." Such an approach can only have negative consequences. Your child has to get the message that you won't deal with him in any way as long as he is screaming.

4. *Let her cry it out.* This is difficult but crucial. Consistency is key. If you walk in or give in, your child knows that she can manipulate you. When you let her cry it out, as unnerving as it may feel, you communicate that you are unwilling to go along with her unreasonable desires. You are in charge.

5. *Use positive reinforcement.* We all bask in the praise of our family, friends, and coworkers. Your child, too, loves to hear your pride in his achievements. Once he has calmed down and is able to hear you, praise his ability to communicate. You can say, "I love it when you tell me with your words what's bothering you. I can really understand you when you're not screaming. Maybe we can find a way to work this out." By paying attention to the positive, you help to eliminate the negative.

SLEEP PROBLEMS

The whole family suffers from sleep deprivation when a child is up at night. Some couples argue about whose turn it is to tend to her. For others, the crying or taking a child into bed interferes with intimacy. You and your wife may also clash, you insisting that the child should cry it out for twenty minutes, your spouse horrified at the thought. In addition, if sleep problems persist, you're apt to be irritable and less able to concentrate at work. Clearly, your toddler's sleep problems cannot be ignored.

While all children resist bedtime once in a while, most are perfectly capable of falling and staying asleep all night. Yet some toddlers habitually refuse to go to bed and vociferously resist sleep by crying in their cribs. Others fall asleep without too much trouble but awaken several times in the night, crying for Mommy or Daddy, their bottle, or a pacifier.

Sleep problems may be in part related to separation anxiety. Bedtime involves your toddler's losing contact with you for several hours. His fears may prevent him from falling asleep or may render him fully awake during a normal period of light sleep. On such occasions, your toddler may cry out in fear or ask to be taken into your bed.

Creating a bedtime ritual that involves quiet play, a reassuring bedtime story, and cuddling will help your toddler make the transition to the land of Nod. This is not the time to engage in roughhousing! Rather, set aside thirty minutes or so before the appointed bedtime for calm, warm, loving activities, and follow a routine that includes pajamas and teeth brushing. Also, alert your toddler five minutes before you're ready to tuck her in. This way, she will become accustomed to the idea of your departure. You can even repeat the same good-night phrase each evening, such as "Nighty-night," "Sleep tight," or "Sweet dreams." Such consistent bedtime rituals help your toddler develop a sense of predictability, trust, and security.

Sleep disturbances may also be learned behavior. In *Solve Your Child's Sleep Problems,* Dr. Richard Ferber, director of the Center for Pediatric Sleep Disorders at Boston Hospital, explains that many sleep problems in young children result from a child's being conditioned to fall asleep in such a way that waking up requires further attention. For instance, if you rock your youngster to sleep, she may have learned to sleep only when held. If you put her down before she's fast asleep, she'll rouse and cry for more rocking. And when she rouses during a period of light sleep, as we all do, she will recognize your absence, become agitated and more fully awake, and finally cry out for further rocking.

Similarly, children who customarily fall asleep while sucking on a bottle or pacifier, or while lying next to you on the couch or in your bed, will resist sleeping without their props—namely, the bottle or *you.* According to Dr. Ferber, your task is to teach the child gently and gradually how to fall asleep alone and how to fall back to sleep if awakened. This means replacing current sleep associations (such as you, a bottle, a pacifier) with more effective ones.

First, introduce a transitional object—a blanket or soft toy—that will be with him when he falls asleep and (unlike you) when he awakens in the middle of the night. It can reassure, soothe, and help him feel safe and in charge of his world. However, it's important to use the blanket or toy consistently. As Dr. Ferber explains, "If you always allow yourself to be used in the manner of such an object—to lie with him, to nurse or rock him . . . to let him twirl your hair whenever he tries to fall asleep—he will never take on a transitional object, because he won't need to."

If the transitional object doesn't bring sufficient relief, you'll want to begin Dr. Ferber's program of retraining the child. Decide in advance how much crying you can tolerate. It may be five, ten, or fifteen minutes. Then go through the child's normal bedtime ritual. If the sleep disturbance revolves around your toddler's need to fall asleep in your arms, this time put him into bed while still awake. Undoubtedly, he'll howl. After five minutes, go in for a minute or two, but don't pick him up no matter how pathetic he looks. Pat him on the back, tell him you love him and aren't going anywhere but that it's time to go to sleep. If your child continues, wait another ten minutes and repeat your reassurances. Finally, wait fifteen minutes between ensuing intervals.

On subsequent evenings, Dr. Ferber recommends increasing the time between visits by five minutes. That is, the second night wait ten minutes before coming in to reassure your child, and fifteen minutes for the second visit. On the third evening, wait fifteen minutes before the first appearance, and so on. Follow the same pattern if your child cries in the middle of the night. After a week or two, the sleep disturbance should subside.

When a demand for late-night feeding causes the awakening, Dr. Ferber suggests reducing the amount of milk in the bottle by an ounce a night, or the time spent nursing by a minute a night, until you reach zero. Although he may have come to expect it, a toddler doesn't need the nightly nutrition. Besides, the additional milk or juice will keep the digestive system working when it should be at rest and will cause extremely wet diapers that may also awaken the child. In all of these relearning techniques, be sure to follow through consistently.

Bringing the toddler into bed with you is not recommended. It can cause resentment between you and your wife, but more important, it's not good for the child. A toddler is busy separating from parents and developing a sense of self. Sharing your bed hinders the process; he needs to sleep alone in order to see himself as a separate person. If your child uses his fears as a way to get into your bed, get to their root rather than jumping at a quick solution. Fear of "monsters" is common at this age. Talking with him about his fears and perhaps consulting a child therapist will help in this regard.

Besides, sooner or later, your toddler will have to learn to sleep alone.

EATING PROBLEMS

During the terrible twos, even eager eaters can become very picky, refusing to try new foods or even to consume old standbys. Other kids get stuck on food favorites—hot dogs or cottage cheese—and won't budge. Often toddlers genuinely don't like the taste of certain foods—broccoli, brussels sprouts, peas, spinach, fish. Indeed, it's wrong if not downright impossible to force a child to eat under any circumstances.

Some children balk at mealtime to get attention, even negative attention. Or they use it to assert their independence: they can control what goes into their mouths, a control they lack in other areas. They may dawdle over dinner, using the old spread-it-around-the-plate trick. Meals can become power struggles if poor eating habits get your goat. You may find yourself suddenly acting the part of cheerleader as you encourage your toddler to "eat so you can grow to be big and strong." In fact, the more you pay attention to it, the worse it gets.

First, realize that your toddler/preschooler won't allow himself to starve to death. Children are self-regulating. Studies have shown that they will take in protein and other needed nutrients over a period of time—days, weeks, or even months—even if they don't eat three balanced meals a day. They may pick at their food for days, then eat more heartily during a growth spurt. And bear in mind that children don't *need* as much food as we often think they do.

Despite genuine concern for your child's health and well-being, it's best to detach yourself from the conflict. Don't let your ego get invested in whether or not your toddler finishes her peas. If she doesn't feel like eating, calmly remove her plate (without such threats as "You'll see, you'll get hungry!") and tell her that if she's not hungry now, she can eat later.

The natural consequence of your child's not eating is hunger. She will learn that soon enough. A toddler needs mid-morning and mid-afternoon snacks, and is often too immature to adhere to a rigid meal schedule. But you can save the leftovers and offer them when she complains of hunger later on. Do avoid sweets and alternative menus, however. If she hasn't snacked inappropriately, you can expect your toddler to eat heartily during the following meal, or the next.

TOILET TRAINING

No congressman is now sitting on Capitol Hill in diapers. We all get the hang of it. Yet some fathers, because of their need to achieve or to control, may push a toddler into toilet training before he is ready, or may react with anger to unintentional pants wetting.

This is not constructive. It only creates power struggles and balkiness. Even a "ready" child who feels pressured may resist, thereby triggering a vicious cycle in which your anger and criticism diminish his feelings of self-worth.

How do you know when your toddler is ready for toilet training? The mental awareness and developmental ability to relate the sensation of a full bladder or bulging bowel to the need to sit on the potty occur between the ages of twenty months and three years. Girls tend to toilet train earlier. In *Toilet Training in Less Than a Day,* learning specialists Nathan H. Azrin and Richard M. Foxx suggest that toilet training is feasible when a toddler

• Has bladder control: can hold urine for several hours instead of dribbling all day long, and shows an awareness, through body language or facial expressions, that he is urinating.
• Is physically ready: has enough coordination to walk across a room or pull down his own pants without parental assistance.
• Can follow instructions: is able to point to various parts of his body, imitate simple games, bring a toy, or put a doll into a box at your request.

Azrin and Foxx suggest that when the child meets these criteria, parents should choose a day (say, on a weekend) when they will be able to concentrate without such distractions as TV, phone calls, or social duties. Using an easily emptied potty chair placed on the kitchen floor and a drink-and-wet doll clad in training pants, the toddler practices all of the steps involved in using the potty: sensing wetness or dryness, approaching the potty rapidly, pulling down the doll's pants, sitting it quietly on the potty, "urinating" (you squeeze out the water), wiping (for girls), pulling up the doll's pants, and disposing of the contents of the bowl in the family toilet.

These practice steps occur under careful guidance and with frequent praise and rewards. These should take the form of salty snacks, such as pretzels or chips, and drinks that the child considers special—the more she drinks, the greater her urge to urinate, the more practice she'll get at using the potty when it's her turn.

Having mastered the sequence from "teaching" her doll, the child practices the potty routine herself. She determines whether or not she's wet and is rewarded for that awareness. At each step, the parent lavishes congratulations, even enlisting the aid of family, friends, and heroes. "Big Bird is so proud that you went in the potty!" or "Grandpa thinks you're such a big girl now!" are motivators.

Accidents should be met with your verbal disapproval delivered in an even tone and not *personally* critical. Say, "I'm unhappy that you wet your pants" or "Daddy likes to pee in the toilet so he doesn't have wet pants." Then have her practice approaching the potty some more, especially from different rooms. Azrin and Foxx explain that your attitude should be that "you love your child just as much as ever, even though you dislike wet pants."

The Preschool Years: From Three to Five

As children outgrow toddlerhood, they mercifully become far less obstinate and far more social. Spending time with playmates becomes a basic need. Language skills have grown enormously, enabling them to communicate without resorting to tears or tantrums. Preschoolers are learning how to control their impulses and cooperate with their parents, teachers, and peers. They spend a good deal of time practicing simple skills, such as tying shoelaces, playing with friends, using a crayon, or riding a tricycle. Some may even begin to master the rudiments of reading and writing.

One of the essential tasks of the preschool years is the honing of social skills. During this stage, your child:

• Plays cooperative games that include the sharing of toys and fantasies.
• Enjoys her playmates and is capable of sharing them with others.
• Joins in on an ongoing game.
• Participates in make-believe games (like playing house) and acts out different roles.
• Asks endless questions (including the ubiquitous "Why?") and is genuinely interested in the responses.
• "Catches" behavior from other children—if one five-year-old starts splitting her Oreos and licking the filling, her playmates copy her.
• Boasts about having the "most" and the "best."
• Continues to test your limits.
• Indulges in tall tales. Most preschoolers aren't liars;

they simply have not yet grasped the distinction between the truth and fantasy.
• Uses bathroom language ("You're a doodie face!") as a way to get attention, in fun with playmates, or in anger.

Because intellectual growth becomes more and more apparent during this age, many fathers are drawn to stressing academics with their preschoolers—an inclination that may stem from a man's need to compete and achieve. These fathers may seek out a nursery school that specializes in "reading readiness" or other structured academic activities in order to give their children an intellectual edge.

Although some precocious children naturally take to reading early, caution is recommended. First and foremost, follow your child's lead. If she is genuinely interested in learning how to read and write, there is no harm in encouraging the natural inclination by providing appropriate materials at home. But never force her to participate in academics against her will. It could create early burnout and resistance to future learning, a very high price.

Besides, experts believe that most precocious readers learn not for their own needs but because they want to please their parents. In addition, an early reader's peers will catch up with her by the time they are six or seven. There's really no rush. Moreover, there are many other more enjoyable ways to encourage a preschooler's intellectual development without imposing undue pressure or inappropriate structure.

You would be wise, for instance, to place your preschooler in a nursery school that stresses social interaction rather than academics. At this age, your child's ability to form social relationships is more pivotal to intellectual development than is his ability to read or recite the alphabet. In fact, children who have problems with social skills often have concomitant academic difficulties.

Developmentalists like Marie Winn, who wrote *Children Without Childhood,* have found that too much early "schooling" can interfere with all-important playtime, which in turn may slow overall development. Usually we don't connect the two—work and play—in our minds. But your preschooler learns during playtime. Consider the simple "play" activity of gluing scraps of paper of various sizes, shapes, and colors into a collage. During this seemingly nonacademic activity children

• Begin to appreciate the similarities and differences among bits of paper and organize them accordingly, a fundamental skill for recognizing letters.
• Count the scraps and identify shapes in preparation for doing arithmetic.
• Practice fine motor coordination, essential to writing.
• Learn colors and enjoy creating something that they regard as beautiful.

Best of all, as they fashion their masterpieces, children stockpile, swap, or share; they imitate one another's patterns and designs; and they discuss and compare the results. Many skills are honed while preschoolers play with one another.

Curiosity is another key element of intellectual development. Preschoolers have a refreshing and insatiable wonder about the world. Everything about their environment is new and exciting. Use nature to respond to this curiosity.

For instance, together you can cultivate carrot, radish, or marigold seeds, take a walk in the park or on the beach, investigate a caterpillar's cocoon or an anthill. As you do, talk to your child about the growth cycle and how seeds need sun, water, and nutrients from the soil in order to flourish. Collect seashells and sand crabs. Explain how ants organize their society and so on, according to your own interests, the seasons, and where you live.

Ask plenty of open-ended questions, such as "What do you think would happen if . . . ?" You might even set up simple science experiments, look at an atlas to discover what lies across the ocean, or trap a caterpillar and watch as it makes a cocoon.

It's crucial to talk with your preschooler frequently, so that he learns how to express complex ideas. Encourage him to speak in full sentences, and listen with interest. Answer your preschooler's questions and engage him in real conversations.

This is a great time to share new experiences such as trips to the airport or the zoo, or outings to concerts, the circus, and the children's museum. If you live in the country, visit the city, and if you live in an urban area, try a journey to a farm. Encourage your child to describe what he has just experienced. If you've just come back from a ball game, let her talk about it; she needs the opportunity to express herself. Rather than ordering her around, or trying to make her experience conform to your expectations, ask her what she thinks.

Creativity is another important component of the child's developing intellect. A child whose imagination runs free envisions new ideas about the workings of the world. Such a child may grow into the scientist who makes a creative leap to solve the puzzle of the origin of the universe or the cure of a deadly disease. Playing some of the imagination-based games suggested in Chapter 10 will help.

Oedipal Games: The Five-Year-Old

Between the ages of four and six your preschooler goes through an emotional transformation: what psychoanalysts call the oedipal stage. You may feel confused if suddenly your daughter becomes quite attached to you or your son becomes Mommy's little boy. In fact, your son may reject you, while your daughter succeeds in wrapping you around her finger.

This is normal. At about age five, little boys begin to feel competitive with their fathers. Indeed, they have an instinctual wish to "possess" their mothers and destroy their fathers—the old oedipal struggle. Likewise, five-year-old girls vie with their mothers for Daddy's attention. However, your son or daughter will eventually surrender, realizing that the quest is hopeless, and join forces with the same-sex parent. At this point, children begin to model themselves after that parent—their sex role prototype.

According to child psychiatrist Robert Furman, director of the Cleveland Center for Research in Child Development, fathers have a great deal to do with how successfully the normal transition is accomplished. "When a father fulfills the 'average, expectable' role with his son, one of kindness, pride, and respect," the little boy has a hard time continuing the battle. He "decides to bow to his love of his father and to the reality of the impossibility of his wishes for his mother." The boy incorporates the image of his father and uses it as a springboard for his own identity as a male.

According to Furman, little girls at this age benefit from giving and receiving gifts from their dad. A father should be open to these small tokens of affection. In that way, he "makes their femaleness something prized and respected. He helps further . . . as he can admire and enjoy their efforts at doing the jobs that mother has taught them." These interchanges foster an affectionate and friendly relationship.

How do you deal with this stage in your child's development? To begin with, don't take a son's rejection personally; it's normal. Continue to be a loving father to the best of your abilities. According to Furman, "All the prior years of the father's caring availability pay off for the son when he can master this transitional phase with a healthy identification with his father and thus acquire those attributes of kindness, giving, and caring for another."

Be affectionate toward your daughter, without leading her to believe that her fantasy can be fulfilled. The truth is that she really *can't* have you, and you must gently disillusion her in that regard by saying, "I know you want to marry me, Wendy, but I'm already married. When you grow up, you'll find a nice man to marry, too." There is no reason to be rejecting. Some men fear that their wives will become jealous or grow anxious about sexual implications. Instead of responding to their little girls' overtures, they withdraw, perhaps no longer allowing their daughters to sit on their laps for stories. Unfortunately, that can make a girl feel unloved and unlovable.

It's also advisable to make your five-year-old conscious of his behavior with the following kinds of statements:

- "Danny, I see you want Mommy all to yourself."
- "Mommy and I love each other, Marty, and when you grow up, you'll find a girl to love, too."
- "You like being Daddy's little girl, don't you, Sara?"

It also helps not to apply adult standards. For example, some fathers get worried when their sons become hostile. They take the words, "I hate you!" literally, and view their five-year-old sons as a threat. Perhaps most disturbing, they act as if their wives *do* have another suitor. In this case, it's important to keep in mind that what is developmentally appropriate for a child is inappropriate for an adult.

The Elementary School Years: Ages Six to Eleven

Your grade schooler is busy mastering basic skills: how to read and write, how to ride a bike and hit a baseball, how to make friends and get along with adults. He competes with his friends yet needs to maintain their good will. Among his peers, he struggles between conformity and the expression of autonomy. And he realizes that as hard as he tries, he still cannot be as competent as an adult. At times he may even feel inferior. Your child's task at this age is to develop basic confidence in his abilities.

Because children are easier to relate to at this age, the popular assumption holds that dads now spend more time engaging in sports, hobbies, or academic pursuits with their kids. This belief, however, is unfounded. According to psychologist Michael Lamb, while "fathers may know more about older children than about younger children, they may feel more comfortable and competent, and they may appear more interested, . . . they apparently do not spend more time with their older children." Indeed, research shows their involvement drops from an average of twenty-six minutes a day to only sixteen. Lamb surmises that this may be so because the kids themselves are less interested in spending time with their parents. Peers and siblings become paramount.

In fact, many men express guilt and ambivalence about neglecting their children during this period. They feel that they respond to a child's greater independence by offering *less* time and love. The responsibility for socializing and educating their kids is delegated to the school in a sort of "tag team" arrangement. Many fathers see themselves as adjuncts, merely reinforcing what their kids have learned elsewhere.

Dads rationalize this distancing by pointing out that kids now need less physical care. They also adhere to the commonly held perception that the first five years of life are the most formative. I disagree. Even though kids at this age may seem to need their fathers less, it is more accurate to say that they need them in a different way: to provide support, wisdom born of experience, and direction.

Fathers are also frequently impatient for their school-age youngsters to master the skills that come so easily to adults. Research indicates that boys who have entered the "age of reason," between seven and ten years old, turn to their fathers for guidance and instruction, and develop mentor relationships in learning how to play chess, dribble a basketball, build a treehouse, or perform experiments with a chemistry set.

That being true, I would encourage your understanding

and compassion and advise you to shun impatience, criticism, and anger when your child struggles to accomplish a skill that seems easy to you but is difficult for him. To be supportive but not overbearing, praise each baby step along the way to mastery and focus on your child's effort rather than the outcome of the project. (See the discussion of successive approximations in Chapter 6.)

It's a fine line: too much involvement on your part can impede development. Your child may be working at a task to fulfill your needs, not hers. This interferes with the development of her own thinking style. She may perceive your overinvolvement as intrusive and demanding behavior, and hear your suggestions as criticism. Your need for your child to achieve takes the fun out of the accomplishment.

Children's achievements become so important at this stage because as men we are conditioned to *do* rather than to just *be* ourselves. We often measure ourselves by our productivity—how much money earned, how many points scored, how many fish caught—not by who we are as people.

When we perceive a challenge, such as a child failing a math test, we automatically feel that we have to *do* something about it, like drill those multiplication tables with flash cards and increase the pressure. But sometimes it would be more helpful to just sit and listen to your kids' concerns. Tell them about how tough long division was for you. Validate their feelings by saying, "I understand that it's hard for you, too." I call this *doing by not doing*.

Your supportiveness is important at this age. And so are fun, exploratory kinds of experiences like the following:

• Riding bikes.
• Playing ball.
• Hiking and camping.
• Exploring museums (in short bursts—don't try to cover the Metropolitan Museum in one day).
• Reading books that your child isn't skilled enough to read yet. (These expand vocabulary and present new experiences and ideas that would otherwise be beyond his reach.)

All of these help your child to find his or her interests and develop curiosity and a love for learning.

Developmentally, the age between seven and eleven is known as the *concrete operations* stage. That means that your school-age child sees things literally and understands that although the objects' appearance has changed, the objects remain essentially the same. A five-year-old, for example, will split apart her Oreo cookie and proclaim that she now has two treats, but your seven-year-old will understand that her cookie cache hasn't multiplied. She can also understand that the eight ounces of water in a tall, narrow glass is the same as the eight ounces of water in a short, squat glass. She can think numerically (by doing math word problems), organize objects into classes, and construct mental images of complex actions. The ability to think logically increases rapidly.

This is an important period for moral development. According to the famous Swiss developmentalist Jean Piaget, children between the ages of six and ten look upon rules and laws as absolutes that must be obeyed. Transgressions must be punished. Youngsters this age take the "rules" seriously, whether they're game rules or classroom procedures; they don't question their origin.

This need for rules is an outgrowth of and a compensation for the tumultuous feelings stirred up during the oedipal phase. Following rules helps your child to feel safe. While you may wish to foster moral behavior at this time (by asking such questions as "What would you do in this predicament?" or teaching right from wrong as situations present themselves), bear in mind that at this age, the adherence to rules is a developmental issue that may shift as your child reaches adolescence and begins pushing against family boundaries to form his own identity. Indeed, you may find him rebelling against guidelines and limits that he was happy to observe during this earlier stage.

By adopting age-appropriate expectations and applauding each small success, you can enhance your child's achievement without undermining his or her self-confidence during these formative years.

Adolescence: Twelve Through Nineteen

Adolescence is perhaps the most difficult time of all for children and parents alike. The tasks of the teenage years are forming identities and becoming independent. Your adolescent asks himself constantly, "Who am I?" In trying to develop a sense of self separate from you, he may become rebellious and try out different, peer-directed identities as he begins to make his way in the world. It's hard not to feel rejected and hurt.

The enormous transformations of puberty, with its growth spurts and hormonal changes, can cause profound emotional swings, inability to concentrate, extreme fatigue, pimples, and obsessive self-consciousness. New-found sexuality surges and crests like waves crashing on the shore. No two adolescents go though their growth spurts in exactly the same fashion, so most feel either too mature or too immature to fit in with the crowd.

Adolescence is divided into three phases (early, middle, and late), but because of the wide range of patterns, the ages of these phases are not fixed. For instance, at twelve, our daughter Cherie still played with dolls like a typical grade schooler, while some of her sixth-grade classmates were already deeply involved in blush, brassieres, and boys.

The early adolescent, roughly between the ages of twelve and fourteen, is characterized by the need for peer acceptance. Cliques of thirteen-year-olds dress the same, listen to the same music, and watch the same movies. They seem to move in packs; only the most mature pair off romantically.

Middle adolescents, generally between the ages of fourteen and seventeen, may feel more connected to their peer groups than to their parents. Many have formed deep and even enduring friendships. They explore their values and solve one another's problems in long, "important" conversations. The phone, always vital, becomes even more important. During this period, the majority of teenagers also become sexually aware, engaging in more serious and long-lasting relationships.

The task of the late adolescent, between the ages of seventeen and nineteen (although it can extend to the age of twenty-four), is to become independent. He looks toward college or otherwise living outside the family home as a way to assert his autonomy. He defines himself by vigorously noting how different he is from his parents. Indeed, parents provide an important springboard: late adolescents push away from Mom and Dad in order to soar toward their own adult lives.

Men often go through their own mid-life crisis at just about the same time. Your adolescent son may be approaching the peak of his virility just as you lament the onset of wrinkles, flab, and gray hair. You may fantasize about or even seek the company of a younger woman to bolster self-esteem. If your parents are frail, you may begin facing the painful truth of your own mortality. The one-two punch of your mid-life crisis and your adolescent's inner turmoil can prove explosive.

Indeed, at this time you may call your entire parenting style and value system into question. Were you too permissive? Too controlling? Faced with open rebelliousness, fathers often find themselves wanting to clamp down even harder on their teenagers—if only to regain a sense of control and create some order in their own lives. The conflict escalates.

Teenage sons and their fathers often become embroiled in power struggles over curfew, use of the car, judgment calls (who's right and who's wrong), politics, religion, money, school performance, smoking, drinking, and drug experimentation. Simple discussions can deteriorate into loud arguments that are really about control: as soon as you're right, your son rebels against the loss of independence.

How often have you heard your teenage daughter weep, "But, Daddy, you just don't understand," and thought, "You're wrong, I was a teenager once, too." A feeling of déjà vu overcomes you. You realize that this is a cry for closeness but also the rejection so essential for separation.

Your daughter wants to be understood and yet needs to remain secretive and mysterious.

Don't give up and abdicate responsibility. Your teens want to be let go, but they also want you to show you care about them, a classic double bind. Their behavior demands that you put the brakes on, yet when you do they're angry and resentful. Adolescents need limits as much as younger children do, but the limits should take a new form. The ability to negotiate and reach compromises is vital; you must respect your child's budding autonomy.

In fact, I call this the age of *chronic negotiation*. Negotiation is the clearest way of establishing progress and peace. So much is going on for the whole family, yet resolution is possible. Orient yourselves so that when you have a conflict, for example, ask your adolescent to list what she wants while you list your own needs. This provides a basis for finding common ground.

Your ability to compromise is essential in maintaining your own sense of control and demonstrating your trust in your adolescent while providing him with a feeling of autonomy and dignity. Families often argue over curfew, for instance. Should sixteen-year-old Michael come in at 12:30 or 1 A.M.? Arguments such as these can rage for days. When families come to me with curfew issues, I suggest a middle ground. Why not 12:45? Fifteen minutes is not worth days of battle. Save your energy for more important issues.

Drug and alcohol abuse, on the other hand, is a much more complex issue and does warrant close attention. While some degree of experimentation is expectable and even normal, a teenager who is impairing his ability to function at school and in society needs some kind of help, whether from a trusted school counselor, a minister or other member of the clergy, a therapist, or a twelve-step program. Your involvement, clearly stated limits, and absence of mixed messages (such as "Do what I say, not what I do . . .") are key in resolving teen substance abuse problems.

The ultimate task of parents during adolescence is to let go—to allow autonomy and independence while setting the age-appropriate limits that your child still needs. As we all did, adolescents make mistakes in groping toward adulthood. In fact, mistakes are an essential part of growing up. Your goal is to minimize the damage. If communication breaks down between you, it's often helpful for your teenager to talk to another adult. Don't shy away from seeking professional help yourself if it seems necessary.

8

What About Sexuality?

SEXUAL learning is a lifelong activity that includes developing attitudes about our bodies, learning how to express affection, and formulating morals. But perhaps most important, sexual learning involves the development of our sex role identities: How do we adapt to the culture's basic assumptions about what it means to be a man or a woman? In our culture, for example, men don't wear dresses, mascara, and panty hose, and women, as a rule, don't change their own spark plugs. Such culturally prescribed behaviors may lead to such sex role stereotypes as "Boys are strong and play rough, whereas girls are dependent and nurture dolls."

Men play a vital part in teaching their children these roles, attitudes, and behaviors. As we have seen, research shows that fathers' sex role beliefs and practices clearly influence their sons'. In *Between Father and Child,* Dr. Ronald Levant, the former director of the Fatherhood Project at Boston University, and writer John Kelly make the point that whereas women teach sex roles by modeling traits and behaviors, men play "the paramount role in shaping a child's ideas about male and female behavior. . . . Men actively shape their responses to a child's gender."

Levant gives the example of a father ignoring his three-year-old daughter's adventure with her big brother's Construx set, "but studies show that a three-year-old son caught with big sister's Barbie usually will be rebuked and Barbie quickly removed from his arms." Perhaps fathers are consciously and unconsciously sensitive to sex role identification because they've learned early on the necessity of maintaining a role in the male hierarchy (see Chapter 3).

Although girls' sexual identity develops largely as a result of interactions with their mothers, fathers also significantly influence it. In Levant's example, fathers do so by paying no attention to the behavior they wish to extinguish. For example, they may not interfere in girls' play with traditionally male toys such as trucks, building sets, or action figures. Researchers have also found that being able to talk with their dads about sexual topics helps young women learn about men. And a father's warmth, praise, and positive attention will enhance a girl's self-confidence around other males. These are more active ways of influencing your daughter's sexual identity.

The Early Roots of Sexuality

Sexuality doesn't begin when it is most manifest, during adolescence, but rather at the moment of birth. It is an outgrowth of the early intimacy between parent and child.

According to the developmental psychoanalyst Margaret Mahler, author of *The Psychological Birth of the Human Infant,* at birth, a baby cannot distinguish between himself and his parents (especially his mother). Although physically separate, he is psychologically fused with her, as if still in the womb. The capacity to develop close relationships springs from this early but essential bonding.

Parents respond to their infant's joy or distress by reflecting his emotions in their voices and facial expressions and by tending to his needs consistently. When a baby recognizes his feelings being mirrored, he feels loved and cared for. If his needs are met consistently, he learns basic trust. Bonding and trust are the early ingredients of intimacy and love. A child who has been rejected at this tender age will not have learned how to become intimate.

Over the first five months of life, your child slowly learns to differentiate what is him from what is not him. He sucks on his toes (defining the boundaries of his body), deliberately reaches for a stuffed animal, and recognizes your presence and absence in games such as peekaboo, thereby demonstrating his awareness that he is a separate being. These are his very first steps toward developing a sense of autonomy and selfhood, another important component of intimacy.

As time goes on, your youngster's separate identity strengthens. An individual with a strong identity is able to let go during lovemaking, to feel momentarily boundariless and merged with his or her partner, and then to regain a sense of separateness.

Other Influences on a Child's Sexuality

A 1989 op-ed piece in the *Los Angeles Times* about sex education in the public schools quoted the late child therapist Dr. Bruno Bettelheim. In part, he said:

> Sex education is a continuous process and it begins the moment you are born. It's in how you are bathed, how you are diapered, how you are toilet-trained, in respect for the body, in the notion that bodily feelings are pleasant and that bodily functions are not disgusting. You don't learn about sex from parental nudity or by showering together. That's nonsense. How you feel about sex comes from watching how your parents live together, how they enjoy each other's company, the respect they have for each other. Not from what they do in bed to each other.

Your attitudes, family traditions, culture, religious beliefs and practices, and behaviors all set the stage for, influence, and contribute to your child's emergent sexual self. A group of scientists headed by Dr. E. J. Roberts that studied specific family characteristics found that how you hold and touch, how you practice nudity or modesty, and how the father behaves as a male in the family all impact a child's developing sexuality.

In essence, you teach intimacy in every interaction with your child—when you embrace him or bandage his scraped knee; when you listen to her worries or comb her hair. The quality of your child's sexual experience once he reaches adulthood is the eventual outgrowth of the kind of parental tenderness and love that begins with cuddling as a baby and appropriately progresses through the various developmental stages into your child's adulthood when he or she is capable of engaging in a loving act of intercourse with another human being. (For more on how to help guide your youngster through the developmental phases, see the section below on the stages of sexual development.)

Culture also influences sexual education. Because we feel uncomfortable communicating about sex with our kids, we often rely on our wives to discuss the birds and the bees during preadolescence and later sex education courses in school. R-rated movies, racy novels, girlie or porno magazines, videos, TV, and friends frequently contribute much, often erroneous, sexual information.

About twelve years ago, I studied a multiethnic group of pregnant teenage girls from a variety of socioeconomic settings. I learned just how misinformed adolescents are. For example, the girls in my study believed that one could not become pregnant from having intercourse only once. These thirteen- to seventeen-year-olds saw sexual activity as a status symbol—the ultimate sign of adulthood—and viewed their pregnancy as a means of taking charge of their lives. Often, they had no concept of sexual pleasure or intimacy.

It behooves us as fathers to address this ignorance more directly, early on. In fact, in light of all the issues that sexually active adults face today (birth control options, AIDS, sexually transmitted diseases such as chlamydia and venereal warts, to name a few), it is more important than ever to talk to our kids about sex. But how do we approach our children? Where do we begin?

Fathers' Reluctance to Talk About Sexuality

Discussing sexuality is very important. Studies have shown that by the time youngsters reach college age, they consistently correlate the amount of sexual information transmitted by their parents with how open and warm the parent-child relationship is and how happy they perceive their parents to be with each other. Nevertheless, many men shy away, leaving direct discussions to their wives or the schools. This may happen for a variety of reasons:

- Men may feel that women are more adept at nurturance, intimacy, and emotions.
- They may feel embarrassed or uncomfortable, especially if they fear inadvertently revealing intimate details about their own experiences.
- They may fear that they don't know enough (especially about female issues).
- They may be unsure whether to take an authoritarian or permissive stance.
- They may have a hard time accepting that their children (of either gender and all ages) have sexual feelings.
- They may fear that providing a teenager with sexual information will give a green light to experiment. (The evidence indicates otherwise.)
- They may be home too little to participate in a serious one-on-one discussion about sexuality with their children.
- They may sense their youngsters' embarrassment about

sexuality and feel awkward about intruding on a private experience.

• They may be unclear about what to communicate to their children at any given age.

The following information on children's sexual development should clarify what to expect from your kids and how to guide them.

Stages of Sexual Development

When you know what your child is experiencing and understand some of the surprising and complex attitudes that can arise, you will have more confidence in exploring his or her feelings.

INFANCY

You can't talk to a baby about sex, but from the moment of birth she is absorbing important sexual information. She learns from how you handle her during bathing and diapering, the pleasure you express about bodily feelings, your acceptance of normal bodily functions, and your nurturing caress.

Much of this sort of teaching goes on unconsciously, but you can also address the issue more directly. As mentioned in the previous chapter, infants learn solely through their senses. When you play, you make eye contact with your child. Gently stroke or cuddle your baby to communicate tenderness and love. During a feeding hold your infant on your bare chest, and experience him melting into your body. That sensation of oneness is the essence of bonding and is at the root of the ability to achieve intimacy.

THE TODDLER YEARS

As discussed earlier, bonding in infancy yields to a burgeoning sense of separateness. A toddler expresses her independence and begins to assert control of the world around her. "NO" becomes her favorite word. Toilet training is a key arena. It's a very effective way for your daughter to manifest control over her own body. She may refuse to use the potty as a means of asserting her autonomy. Such declarations of independence are your youngster's way of defining her own identity.

Because toilet training involves an awareness of the genitals, control and letting go, and comfort with one's body—all important elements of physical and sexual development—it's vital to convey to your toddler that normal body functions are not the source of shame or disgust. For example, if your daughter has a toileting accident, rather than scolding her for being "dirty" or showing disgust, say with equanimity, "I see that you didn't make it to the toilet on time. Let's change your pants. Next time, let me know if you need my help."

Toddlers are busy expanding their vocabularies and are apt to use words to refer to their genitals. Although families have been known to give them "pet" names, it seems simplest and least confusing for your youngster to call her reproductive organs by their anatomical names. Of course, as your child matures, she is sure to pick up whatever slang designations are currently in use.

You may also find that your toddler wants you to sleep with her, either by coming into your bed or your going into hers. This is inadvisable for separation reasons (see Chapter 7). In addition, there may be a point at which bringing your child into your bed at night could interfere with intimacy between you and your wife. Of course, a Saturday morning snuggle and giggle session in bed is great fun for all!

PRESCHOOL: AGES THREE TO FIVE

Ages three to five are years of intense sexual curiosity, when bathroom talk is riotously funny and children want to know where they come from, and when family patterns of behavior are established. Preschoolers are busy exploring the world around them, including their bodies and their physical sensations. Some preschoolers don't stop with their own bodies, going on to check out their playmates or siblings. "Doctor" games are common. This is quite normal sexually innocent play that results from your child's natural curiosity.

In *The Right to Innocence*, Los Angeles child sexual abuse specialist Beverly Engel explains that normal sexual exploration games between "consenting peers" occurs "only between those of the same age, sexual experience, and power." (Sexual activity between a preschooler and school-age or adolescent child is sexual abuse.) If you walk in on imaginative sex play among consenting preschoolers, it's best not to respond with disgust or to shame the children into stopping. Such a reaction may cause the kids to feel that they have done something terrible, that sexual matters or certain parts of the body are "dirty" or "wrong." This attitude could have lifelong consequences, impairing or preventing your child's eventual sexual enjoyment.

You might say, "I know you guys are curious about your bodies, but your penises/vaginas [or whatever other term your family uses to describe genitals] are private. I'd be happy to answer any questions that you may have." Your preschooler has to explore. Your role is to teach socially acceptable parameters such as telling your child that it's okay to touch his own genitals in the privacy of his bedroom or bathroom but it's not okay to touch them in public or to touch someone else's.

You also can expect "Where did I come from?" questions at this age. Welcome these queries and answer them straightforwardly. A preschooler is capable of understanding the mechanics of reproduction within the context of a loving relationship. Reading and discussing books about the conception and birth of baby animals and humans can be useful, especially if your wife is pregnant. *Where Did I Come From?*, a picture book by Peter Mayle and Arthur Robins, is entertaining and informative.

THE OEDIPAL STAGE

At about five years of age, your child goes through what may be a confusing stage for you. Eleanor may suddenly act "seductive"; she climbs on your lap for hugging and kissing every time you sit down. Or Jack may pound on your legs whenever you and your wife embrace. As explained in

Chapter 7, at this age, a subconscious desire to possess the opposite-sex parent and even destroy the same-sex parent comes forward.

Often five-year-olds will ask their opposite-sex parents, "Do you love me more than anyone else in the world?" When you say yes, they'll come back with, "So why are you always kissing Mommy (or Daddy)?" These are very normal expressions of jealous but unfulfillable longings.

It's important to respond to your five-year-old daughter's intimacy needs but *not* to their "sexual" aspect. For example, you can say, "I love you equally but in different ways, Eleanor. I've got enough love for everyone including you, Mommy, and Timmy." You can stroke her hair and listen to what's on her mind, laugh, and have your private jokes. But do not further encourage her approaches. There's a difference between affectionate warmth and a sexual response, and your instinct will help guide you. A sexual response involves overt stimulating behavior, such as kissing your daughter on the neck or other erogenous zone, or covert behavior, such as commenting that her body is sexually desirable. (Inappropriate behavior is discussed further on page 196.) It is essential to be physically affectionate with your daughter, without sexual overtones.

If you feel confused or nervous, just make certain to reassure her of your love, broken-record style. Every time she questions your affection for your wife you can repeat, "I love you, Eleanor, but I love you differently than Mommy." Then channel her feelings into affectionate activities, such as coloring together, reading a favorite story, or going for a bike ride. When Eleanor realizes that her quest is hopeless, she will begin her long stride toward autonomous adulthood and appropriate sexual partners.

As far as your son is concerned, there is no reason for you to feel rejected, jealous, or hurt. Reassure him that when you kiss Mom, it doesn't hurt her. You can add, "I know you want to be with Mommy now. When we're finished hugging, we'll hug you, too." Your role is to establish appropriate parameters here, making sure not to rebuff Jack but also making it quite clear that Mommy is married to you. You can try what we used to call a "huggie sandwich," with Mom and Dad on the outside and child or children in the middle, all hugging.

THE LATENCY STAGE: AGES SIX TO ELEVEN

At the beginning of the elementary school years, your child's sexual desires will go underground. The energy now goes toward same-sex friendships, interest in competition and achievements, and adherence to the rules of fairness.

Psychologists call this normal process *sublimation*. This means that Frank will be much more interested in following rules, be they moral dicta or the fine print of a Monopoly game, than he was as a preschooler. In general, rules are important at this age because they compensate for and control the impulses that seemed to have taken over during the oedipal stage. Your child respects rules and finally understands the difference between right and wrong. Tattling and cries of "cheater" are the hallmark of this stage. At this time, the child needs rules and limits to be honored, a structure that provides a sense of containment, and safety.

As an outgrowth of their new alliance with the same-sex parent, school-age children will suddenly appear disgusted by members of the opposite sex. "Girls? Yuck!" "Boys? Who needs them?" Now, boys become their dads' sports buddies and girls play house, office, or school.

Toward the end of latency, between the ages of nine and eleven, your child is mastering the basic skills of friendship. He or she will most likely form an intense relationship with a "best friend" of the same sex. According to psychiatrist Harry Stack Sullivan, friends at this age experiment with intimacy and learn behavior patterns that shape later intimate relationships. They share secrets, talk about what they understand sex to be, and look at sexually explicit books and photographs. You may also discover latency-age children in sex exploration play, normally only between same-sex, same-age youngsters.

Privacy becomes a big issue now, too. Before, you or your wife might have felt free to bathe Anna; now she may lock the bathroom door. She may develop crushes on boys but refuse to talk about them, or keep a secret diary. She may have even become terribly shy or uncomfortable about her body, resisting her mother's intervention in the department store dressing room or the doctor during a medical examination.

Modesty often intensifies during preadolescence, as bodies begin to change. Honor your latency-age child's need for privacy. It validates her sense of independence by conveying your appreciation for the fact that her body, thoughts, and feelings are her own. Make sure to knock on her door, and wait for her response before entering. Respect her need to take care of or be private about her own body. Also, avoid teasing her or drawing attention to her changing figure for she's probably terribly self-conscious about it. Instead, focus on the positive, telling her what a great haircut she just got, or that a certain color suits her perfectly.

The latency period lasts until the onset of puberty, sometime between the ages of ten and fourteen.

ADOLESCENCE

Adolescence is tumultuous. Your child's goal is to define herself as separate and different from you. In the process, she tries on a variety of personalities in order to find the one that suits her. From one month to the next she may embrace various modes of dress, favorite music (from rap to punk to heavy metal and back to rap again, or whatever the latest craze is), corresponding hairdo, and a variety of steady boyfriends. This process, disconcerting as it may be for you as a parent, is an important step toward adulthood.

According to the famed developmentalist Erik Erikson, the successful resolution of this identity crisis is crucial for the ability to create true intimacy with another person during early adulthood. Intimacy is based on a healthy sense of self, which is arrived at via these many shifts and experiments. Only after having established a strong identity can an adolescent become truly close with another.

A teenager whose identity is still in flux may therefore experience roller-coaster relationships, short-lived but intense or long-lived and subject to peaks and valleys. Often adolescents are confused about what love is and how to define a true friend. Besides, intimacy is risky business; many teenagers and young adults feel too insecure to make the leap into another's world.

Because of these swings, it is often more comfortable for younger teenagers to go out in groups of friends, so that intense emotions can be dissipated. A crowd of boys may meet a clique of girls at parties, dances, the movies, or the mall. Their flirting interactions are the beginnings of future, private activities such as long conversations, dating, intimacy, and sexual experimentation. "Going steady" can run like an epidemic through a group of young adolescents; if two classmates have coupled up, everyone else in the crowd needs a "steady," too.

Messages from parents, family, peers, or the media shape your teenager's attitudes toward sexual activity. If, for example, parents are comfortable with open displays of physical affection, their adolescent children naturally incorporate this style into their own relationships. Other families may be more reserved in their expression, and their children may react by adopting that pattern or by rebelling against it as a way to declare their independence.

Every teenager is both eager for and afraid of sexual experience. Indeed, sometimes adolescents will experience both an urgency for and a fear of intimacy within moments of each other.

How should a father respond? It's important to follow your adolescent's lead, for she's sure to give you cues. For example, your thirteen-year-old daughter may flatly prohibit conversation about her boyfriend and comments regarding her appearance. In order to preserve her trust, respect her wishes. This, in turn, will help her feel more comfortable and successful in setting limits with boys.

Rather than feeling resentful, or pressing the issue, you can ask, "Tell me, Stacy, what's okay for us to talk about now that you're growing up?" or "How can I let you know how beautiful I think you're becoming without embarrassing you?" Unfortunately, many dads withdraw from their daughters at this sensitive age. They feel embarrassed by their girls' attractive and womanly bodies and are unsure of how to relate. If they do comment on the changes, their daughters may respond with fury and humiliation. The truth is, adolescent girls still need contact with their dads. Let your child know that you're open and willing to talk to her whenever *she* feels ready. And when she does come to you with a question or problem, do your best to be available. Use active listening, mirroring, and eye contact to let her know that you respect her feelings and perspective (see page 120).

Even though your teenage daughter still needs your affection, its manifestation may become less physical. I knew my daughters had reached adolescence when they started giving me what I called "A-frame hugs." That is, they were only embracing me from the neck up; our bodies seemed miles apart. Full-body hugs are now reserved for eligible males of their own generation. This felt like a loss but an appropriate and necessary one.

Your daughter benefits from discussing dating, boyfriends, intimacy, and sexuality with you. It helps her understand how men think, and it helps her resist sex role stereotypes in which women are expected to defer to men.

When it comes to your teenage son, you may feel an underlying sense of competition as he strives to prove himself in his own eyes. Try to get beyond this, because, like daughters, sons need their dad's support in dealing with puberty's physical and emotional changes. Though boys are less likely to want to hide their bodies from their fathers, they're still concerned about physical development and attractiveness. Early adolescence can be especially awkward. Pimples, uneven growth spurts, and delayed development all undermine self-confidence. Your son may also begin experiencing erections at inopportune moments and may feel embarrassed by this uncontrollable display of emerging sexual identity.

Talking with your teenage son about sex and about competitiveness with his friends helps him feel less pressured, especially if he's a late bloomer. Yet even early bloomers may need special attention. Although their emotional maturation may lag far behind, physically developed boys may feel thrust into social situations such as dating or intimacy that they are as yet unable to handle or understand emotionally. Help your son to see that even though he may be feeling pressured to prove himself with girls, it's okay (and perhaps in his best interest) for him to take his time.

Finally, for their own protection, a discussion of birth control options and responsibilities, AIDS, and sexually transmitted diseases should be part of your dialogue with young adolescents of both genders. To obtain free educational pamphlets about birth control options, AIDS, and other sexually transmitted diseases (including how to prevent diseases such as genital herpes, gonorrhea, chlamydia, and genital warts), send a note specifying which pamphlets you want and a self-addressed stamped business-size envelope to the American College of Obstetrics and Gynecology, Resource Center, 409 12th Street, S.W., Washington, D.C. 20024-2188. You can also call the National AIDS Hotline at 1-800-342-AIDS or the National Sexually Transmitted Diseases Hotline at 1-800-227-8922 for advice and educational materials.

Touching

A common concern for fathers of boys is whether a lot of physical contact with a son will "cause" the boy to become gay. With daughters, there is anxiety about their own sexual arousal or their wives potential jealousy.

You will be happy to know that there are no limits to the benefits of *appropriate* touch. You can hold seven-year-old Jessica on your lap, for instance, while reading the paper, watching TV, or telling a bedtime story and she will benefit. And, rather than "rendering" your son gay, your warmth and affection will reinforce his good feelings about you.

Gauging how much touch feels right involves several issues. First, evaluate your family's approach to physical contact. Are you comfortable touching one another? How do you feel about hugging and kissing your wife in front of friends or family? Do you hold hands naturally in the course of the day? Do you hug and/or kiss your kids when they get home? Do you roughhouse with them? Do they feel comfortable crawling into your lap? These attitudes about touch are unconsciously communicated to your children.

Next, consider your child's temperament and disposition. Some kids like a lot of physical contact, while others need more distance. Often, touch may depend on mood, both yours and your child's. Neither of you may want physical contact when preoccupied with other matters. It's important to respect one another's limits.

In fact, when it comes to hugging and touch, I would advise you to follow your child's lead as if you were dancing with him. Many men are used to being the one in charge, but in this instance, your child should show you the way, because his control of the situation helps him to feel safe and to maintain the boundaries of his identity. If he calls the shots, he will feel less invaded by your needs. Indeed, the amount of touching between you and your youngster may be less important than how mutually satisfying it is to both of you.

Over the last decade our culture has become increasingly sensitized to the issue of child sexual abuse. Of course, this is important and positive, but it has had the unfortunate side effect of frightening many men away from physical contact, however appropriate, with their children. Sadly, this kind of withdrawal deprives kids of vital love and attention. Children often learn about their sexual identities from how their fathers respond to them.

The vast majority of families enjoy a good deal of physical touching without even a hint of sexual threat. The line between affectionate play and overt or even covert sexuality is clear and constant. Indeed, the awareness of that "line" allows for great freedom in family contact, closeness, and touching.

You communicate a feeling of safety to your child by respecting his or her privacy and body and by setting clear guidelines as to what is acceptable and what is unacceptable play. (In the next section, I'll cover specifically what constitutes unacceptable behavior.) There is no inherent reason that you can't hug and love your kid—as long as you're not invasive or conveying a double message. For example, tickling can be a great giggle-provoking roughhouse experience but it can also go too far, becoming emotionally hurtful and physically painful when your child's limits aren't respected. In essence, safety means stopping physical contact when your child asks you to.

What Constitutes Sexual Abuse

On the other hand, the guidelines for what constitutes inappropriate sexual touch are quite clear. You might be surprised to learn that many forms of sexual abuse do not involve actual intercourse or penetration. According to psychotherapist Beverly Engel, author of *The Right to Innocence: Healing the Trauma of Childhood Sexual Abuse* and the director of the Center for Adult Survivors of Sexual Abuse, "Many victims of sexual abuse don't know they are victims, because they don't realize what happened to them was in fact sexual abuse. Some are still under the misconception that they weren't sexually abused unless they were actually penetrated or forced." According to Engel, who is an incest survivor herself, childhood sexual abuse includes any interaction between a child and an adult when the child is being used as an object of gratification for adult sexual needs or desires.

In *Handbook of Clinical Intervention in Child Sexual Abuse*, Suzanne M. Sgroi lists the following absolutely inappropriate abusive adult behaviors (besides intercourse):

• *Approach behavior:* any indirect or direct sexual suggestion, including sexual looks, innuendos, or suggestive gestures.
• *Nudity:* deliberately parading around the house in front of family members (see below).
• *Disrobing:* getting undressed in front of the child when the two of you are alone.
• *Genital exposure:* exposing the genitals and directing the child's attention to them.
• *Observation of the child:* surreptitiously or overtly

watching the child undressing, bathing, or using the toilet.
* *Kissing:* kissing in a lingering or intimate way.
* *Fondling:* caressing breasts, abdomen, genital area, inner thighs, or buttocks. The child may similarly fondle the adult at his request.

Obviously, any form of genital touching, masturbation, or oral, anal, or genital intercourse is also strictly off limits.

It is not uncommon for fathers to be sexually aroused by their daughters at most ages. Everyone has fantasies of one kind or another. You tread dangerous ground only if you want to act on them. If you're having difficulty controlling your behavior, seek help from a competent psychotherapist before your impulses become a problem that could cripple your child emotionally.

Often sexual feelings expressed toward a son or daughter are the result of conflicts in the marriage. If intimacy levels have deteriorated, sexual feelings can get displaced. Under these circumstances, counseling is strongly recommended.

It is important for fathers to teach children from toddlerhood onward that their bodies are their own property. We often stress to our kids that they shouldn't talk to strangers, but we rarely teach them how to protect themselves from people they do know—and most abusers, like most rapists, are known by the victim.

Adults often unwittingly intrude upon children's bodies in subtle and even loving ways. Your friends and acquaintances may pick up Matthew, cuddle him, or pinch his cheeks without ever asking him if that's okay. These largely well-meaning but ill-informed people operate under the assumption that adults can do whatever they want with kids.

To understand why this can be frightening, try putting yourself in your son's shoes. Uncle Charlie is three times as big as him, has a booming voice, and smells of cigar smoke. Unless Matthew really wants to be held by his uncle, he may feel too intimidated to resist. It would be your job, then, to intervene and let Charlie know that Matthew doesn't want to be held. In your absence, you might want to prepare Matthew in advance. Teach him that he is in charge of his own body and that if he doesn't want to be held, he can say no. You could rehearse such phrases as: "I don't want to be picked up." "Please don't touch me." "You hurt me when you pinch me. Please stop." "My body is my own property."

Your child's eventual ability to achieve intimacy is connected to his feelings of emotional trust and bodily safety. He equates physical protection with emotional security because when he's safe, he knows that his boundaries and limits will be respected. The ability to let go during intimacy is linked to feeling safe within one's boundaries.

Nudity and Privacy

As with touch, there are no hard-and-fast rules about nudity and privacy. In some families people undress only behind locked doors. In other households, however, occasional nudity occurs naturally, without attracting much attention. If you are comfortable with your body, you will communicate that attitude to your child.

You and your son can be naked together at any age. On the other hand, your daughter's temperament and stage of development may affect her feelings about being naked around you or seeing you undressed. Toddlers have little modesty and may pull off their clothes at a moment's notice to roll in the mud or run through the sprinklers on a hot summer day. As long as the activity is not sexualized (see preceding section), you can bathe or shower with your toddler with no ill effect, and even check out the chicken pox on her vagina that she wants to show you.

As a girl grows from toddler to preschooler, however, she becomes more aware of the differences in male and female anatomy. She may stop taking showers with you and may insist on bathing herself. This is your clue that being nude with each other in a regular (not haphazard) fashion is no longer comfortable for her. When she pointedly remarks on your nudity with statements such as "Ooh, daddy. You're naked!" it may be her way of telling you she no longer feels comfortable seeing you undressed. It's time to follow her lead.

What to do in cases of accidental exposure? Think of them as perfect opportunities to teach your youngster about privacy. Trust your instincts on this. Should you walk in on your naked child, you can back out with a quick "Excuse me. I didn't mean to intrude." If your daughter should come upon you as you're getting out of the shower, you can say, "I prefer that you don't come in when I'm naked. Next time, please knock. Wait for me to tell you when I'm ready." Comment neutrally lest your child get the feeling that bodies are disgusting or shameful, or she has done something terribly wrong. Make sure not to overreact by getting angry or yelling.

If your child makes a habit of catching you undressed, she may be trying to satisfy a natural curiosity. That may be your cue to set up a discussion about reproduction and anatomy. You might begin your talk by saying, "I've noticed that you've been coming into my room when I'm naked. Do you have any questions about my body?" Focus on what your child is curious about. It would also be a great time to read *Where Did I Come From?* or, for the latency-age and preadolescent child, *What's Happening to Me?*, both by Peter Mayle and Arthur Robins.

In this chapter, I have given you some guidelines to help shape your interactions and discussions with your children and to temper your own judgments regarding their sexual development. This chapter can also be part of a useful discussion with your wife. Airing your individual views on touching, privacy, and nudity can help you clarify your positions with each other, enabling you to set consistent and appropriate parameters with your kids that benefit family closeness. Together, you can map out your views. Your children's sexual development can become a source of conflict, but by addressing the issues we've raised early on, it can also be a source of intimacy. If your values differ significantly, negotiate with one another or seek professional help—from a member of the clergy or a therapist—to assist you in working out an approach that the whole family can live with.

Throughout the last four chapters, I have provided tools to enhance your understanding of your impact on your children's overall growth and development. Part 3 of *Finding Time for Fathering* will introduce you to the many games and activities in which you can become engaged.

PART 3

Finding the Time: How to Get Involved With Your Children

9

A Word on Quality Time

RECENTLY, while observing two families eating brunch at a favorite local restaurant, I was struck by the disparity in interactions between fathers and children. The first couple came to breakfast with their three-year-old and their copy of the Sunday *New York Times*. It seemed as if they wanted to be with their child, yet they also needed some time off. And so they read their paper and indulged their youngster in a passive way, allowing her to climb all over them and the booth while exclaiming about her cuteness. Yet, despite their affection, they hardly paid attention to their little girl or engaged her in activities that intensified their connection. This was their opportunity to read the Sunday paper, and they weren't relinquishing it.

Predictably, this preschooler resorted to increasingly silly behavior to gain her parents' full attention: she balanced herself on top of the booth and then slid off; she ran amok among the tables, engaging the other patrons and causing the waiters to navigate around her. Finally, her dad retrieved her and helped her eat her pancakes.

Although it's true that this couple had taken their daughter out to breakfast, one could not honestly say that they had spent much "quality" or any other kind of time with her. This dad had missed an opportunity to find time for fathering. Perhaps spending five minutes looking at the pictures in the magazine might have been enough to make a meaningful connection with his daughter.

The following Sunday: same restaurant, different dad and three-year-old. This man seemed to understand the meaning of the term "quality time." While father and daughter awaited the arrival of their pancakes, this second father decided to make a puppet out of an extra paper napkin on the table. He tied knots in two corners (to form long, pointy ears) and exclaimed to his daughter that "Bunny" had come to eat breakfast with them. Indeed, Bunny kept the preschooler and her dad gleefully entertained not only before but also during and after breakfast.

This father had used creatively the little time he and his daughter had together to maximize their good feelings toward one another and to get into each other's fantasy world. He had used their time together for fathering and as a result, they had had a "quality" interaction.

Is It a Matter of Time?

I am often asked the following questions:

- Is more time together inherently better than less?
- Does the time have to be regularly scheduled?
- Is one full day a month better than fifteen minutes snatched here and there during the week?
- Is "quality time" a myth to ease my conscience, or can it be made into a reality?

• If I can't give less to my career and I can't find another hour in the day, exactly how can I find the time for fathering?

Although the answers are as individual as each family situation, generally the question of *how much* time is overshadowed by the equally important issue of how you choose to spend the time you do have. What follows are some general principles to help structure your involvement with your children.

1. *More time is better than less—but it needs to be the right kind of time.* What you do during your time together—the quality of your interactions—is as important as the amount of time you spend. The principles of authoritative fathering apply here: express warmth and affection to your kids while conveying appropriate limits and expectations.

   Going back to the observations in the restaurant, even if the first father had allocated twelve hours with his daughter, had they continued their present level of involvement they would have been no closer or happier at the end of a full day together. This dad was alternately permissive, preoccupied, and frustrated, while his daughter's behavior was both a cry for attention and an indication that her parents had forestalled their responsibility to set limits on her behavior (see Chapter 6). Sure, more time is better than less (and some is better than none at all), but only if you're actively and positively involved with your kids.

2. *Schedule time together regularly, if you can.* Predictable playtimes, such as storytelling ten minutes before bed-

time each night, Saturday mornings gluing model airplanes or playing tennis together, or Tuesday evenings
spotting cartwheels for your budding gymnast, create a
ritual of interactions that can help your youngsters feel
secure. With regularly scheduled activities, kids know
that they can depend on you to be available when you say
you will and they look forward to your time together.

3. *In the absence of a regular schedule, set up appointments to
play.* If your work or other demands preclude creating
such rituals, let your youngsters know that although you
can't set up a formal routine, you will spend time with
them. Then, make a date. You could say, for example,
"Next Sunday, let's go to the batting cages before lunch
so you can practice your swing," or "Tomorrow night, I'll
be able to color with you after dinner." Even stopping off
for a promised frozen yogurt on the way home from the
cleaners can be a special time. You'll all anticipate the
activity. Just make sure to follow through without distraction. In Chapters 11 and 12 I'll show you some ways to
keep the contact going with your kids, even if you're at
work or must be absent from the home.

4. *The quality of your interaction may be more important than the
amount of time devoted to an activity.* Is one day a month
better than fifteen minutes here and there? Again, that
depends. Fifteen minutes of daily ridiculing is about
equal to a full day of criticism once a month. Neither will
do much for your youngsters' self-esteem or your relationship. If one day a month is all you can allot, then
make the most of it.

For example, if you choose to take your kids to an
amusement park on your day together, pay attention to
the quality of your interactions. How do you use the drive

to the park? Do you talk about things that matter to your kids, or are you preoccupied with business concerns? What do you do while standing in line waiting for the rides? Do you sing songs, tell jokes, play "I Spy," and make up stories and word games, or do you all stand around in stony silence? If you never talk to one another, your outing together will simply increase everyone's feelings of loneliness. That's not quality time. Playing, talking, singing, and giggling are.

5. *Quality time doesn't have to be extraordinary.* Positive fathering interactions can occur during routine, everyday activities. Sometimes, just being aware that the ten minutes spent in the car on the way home from the sitter is an opportunity for play can open new possibilities for you and your children. Even caretaking chores can be an opportunity for fun and intimacy: play a counting game as you button shirts or slice carrots. Besides, if you have only fifteen or twenty minutes a day with your kids, you might as well engage in games and diversions that help draw you closer (see Chapter 10).

6. *Be appropriately democratic.* Quality time is often a matter of how you, as a family, decide which activities to enjoy. One family set aside one Saturday each month for a family activity. Each member got his or her turn to choose what the family would do—the beach one month, a concert the next, ice skating the third. Each member had the opportunity to feel empowered and important, and consequently they all had a good time.

Think about how your family chooses the rides at the amusement park, for example. Does each person get to pick a favorite (even if you have to go on the kiddie rides once in a while), or do you hand down the decrees about which rides will be taken? If some rides are dangerous for young children, allow your youngsters to choose among those that are safe for them.

If your children never get a turn to pick the activity, they will be deprived of the opportunity to make decisions and may balk at your authoritarian attitude. Rather than having fun, you may all become embroiled in a power struggle.

7. *Respect your youngsters' limitations.* In general, in order to have quality time you must have realistic expectations of each child's abilities and attention span. Otherwise you may impose your agenda (to see everything in the park, to get your money's worth, to have your own good time) on children too immature to handle it. Fortunately, the more you're involved in your youngsters' lives, the more sensitive you will be to their cues, capabilities, and interests. That's one of the hidden advantages of spending time together.

Your children may become overstimulated and cranky long before you're ready to leave a family attraction. It's not much fun to drag screaming or whining children around Disneyland, the zoo, or a day hike. What to do in this situation? Keep the activity short and sweet. You may find it necessary to curtail the outing—even while you're all still having fun—with a promise to come back next month or next season. Despite the fact that you've doled out a lot of money in entrance fees, it won't do you or your children any good if you insist on staying long after they have exhausted themselves.

Is "Quality Time" a Myth?

In the best of all possible worlds, we would spend great quantities of quality time with our kids. Knowing that most of us don't have that luxury shouldn't dissuade us, however, from making the most of the snippets of time that we do have together. Finding time for fathering doesn't necessarily mean manufacturing more time. Rather, it means using moments together (say, when you're getting your youngsters ready for school or waiting for your hamburgers at McDonald's) more enjoyably.

In the next three chapters, I'll be sharing activities, games, attitudes, and approaches that will help you maximize what little time you do have with your kids. Chapter 10 explains how to play *noncompetitively* with your youngsters so that they allow you into their world and you allow them into yours. While not meant to be an encyclopedic compendium of all the activities fathers can share with their kids, Chapter 10 will teach you an approach to interaction that you can apply to all of your activities.

In Chapter 11 we'll explore how to incorporate your children into your work world so that it no longer seems to them like an alien experience. We'll also examine balancing fathering with work if you operate your business from home. In Chapter 12 I'll help you to find ways to maintain a connection with your kids even if business travel, divorce, vacations, and boarding school keep you separated from one another.

Finding time for fathering is not about making more demands on you. Rather, it's about becoming aware of hundreds of opportunities to interact meaningfully with your kids—opportunities that exist within your family everyday. Quality time is not a myth, but it must be present in sufficient quantities to make a positive impact on your relationship with your kids.

10

How to Play With Your Children

WHY do you play with your youngsters? I'll bet your first response is that it's lots of fun. And you're right. Play is a great way for everyone to have a good time. But play has other advantages, as well. It provides an opportunity for physical and emotional contact with your children and teaches them about the world. When you play with your kids, you create deep bonds of closeness.

Men nurture their kids naturally during playtime experiences. Often "games" between men and their children involve competition or the achievement of certain preset goals: who'll score the most baskets, build the highest tower of blocks, bat in the most runs, complete the most airplane models, or amass the most money (with hotels on Boardwalk and Park Place) in Monopoly. Competition doesn't have to be cutthroat; it can be fun, challenging, and stimulating. It can teach children valuable lessons, including:

• Sometimes you win and sometimes you lose.
• Social situations may be structured in hierarchies; being able to work well in a given system may include being able to recognize rank and position.

- In some pursuits, the capacity to accomplish tasks and meet or beat deadlines is highly valued.
- Persistence, tenacity, and hard work can pay off.
- One can depend on one's teammates/playmates to help accomplish a goal.

Remembering that the authoritative father expresses high expectations coupled with warmth, we can see how competitive play meshes with the high expectations side of the authoritative equation. We want our kids to win or at least do their best in a competitive endeavor.

Indeed, we often base our fathering activities on competition. We coach soccer teams or play chess, we take our kids to the ball game or beat them at thumb wrestling. This occurs because as boys, we were socialized to think hierarchically: if someone's on top, then someone else is on the bottom. Competition was built into our play activities, and now it permeates our interactions with our children from infancy to adulthood. (Many new fathers buy their infant boys footballs or baseball logo rompers in anticipation of competitions to come!)

But while competitive play can be exciting and instructive, it can also build walls between us and our children. During competition, we tend to focus on the result rather than the person and her process. Sometimes criticism creeps in; winning or losing can become more important than our children's feelings. Goals must be met at all costs, or what's the sense of playing? The truth is, competition and the need for achievement can infuse play interactions with a certain tension and stress for you as well as for your children. Sometimes we must be on guard for negative attitudes because we've been conditioned to be critical.

The Virtues of Noncompetitive Play

Noncompetitive play, on the other hand, addresses the warmth side of the authoritative father equation. You emphasize your child's effort, not necessarily the result. Stress diminishes when you dwell on the process (how your child approaches a situation) of play rather than the goal. In noncompetitive play, there are no winners or losers, only people cooperating, getting close, and having fun.

During noncompetitive play you can

* Teach about your own life.
* Learn how your youngsters perceive their world.
* Interact creatively and use ordinary, commonly available play materials.
* Include your kids in your hobbies.
* Enhance family intimacy.
* Have lots of fun.

Although men are often great at competitive games, many of us have little experience in noncompetitive activities. So, rather than listing the obvious activities in which dads engage, such as coaching teams, playing sports, or practicing competitive skills, in this chapter I will help you explore this other form of meaningful play that promotes closeness and helps produce bright, successful, and creative kids.

The chapter is divided roughly into four sections: activities from birth to age five, activities for school-age kids, approaches for adolescents, and strategies to make competitive games more enjoyable. Bear in mind that some of the age divisions are artificial. Although your ten-year-old may be embarrassed by a "silly daddy," you can still read to him (books like *Tom Sawyer* or *Charlie and the Chocolate Factory*) and you can certainly introduce your youngster to the joys of camping and fishing or museums long before he starts school. What follows are simply general guidelines.

Preschoolers

USING BOOKS

Many fathers are determined to get to the end of the bed-time story, no matter what. They may ignore their youngsters' questions and push ahead, missing valuable opportunities for intimacy and insight into their kids' attitudes and perceptions. During one workshop, Steve recounted finding himself reading faster and faster as the story progressed. His heart began to pound, quickening with the pace. The other dads reported similar experiences. Most of them thought reading to their kids was fun, but there were days when it just seemed like another *job*.

To eliminate the pressured feeling, why not read creatively in ways that don't involve achievement? For instance, discussing pictures or text may be more significant for your kids than the completion of the tale itself. Asking them to imagine what the story is about from the pictures or the title page engages their imagination while you learn how they think. Such positive interactions benefit intellectual development, creativity, flexible thinking, and all aspects of achievement in the long term.

Through active storytelling you can help your children

- Express ideas and feelings.
- Increase their vocabulary and enrich thought processes.
- Learn how to struggle through complex ideas.
- Give free rein to their imagination.

Furthermore, your kids feel listened to and valued. Rushing to the end of the story is not the point. Spending warm, loving time together is.

To reveal how a youngster perceives the world, and to bring you closer, try these reading techniques.

1. *Make storytime a fun time.* Set aside ten to fifteen minutes daily for stories. (If you're not home in the evening at bedtime, try it in the morning.) Just make sure you're not interrupted—this is special time. Cuddle up together. Put your arm around your child. Storytime should be a special part of the day when you share warmth and love.
2. *Get your child involved in the story.* Rather than fixing your sights on the end of the tale, try just meandering through it. Have Jason look at the pictures and make up his own story to go with them. This motivates him and activates his imagination. Try a book without words (many such picture books are available) and make up a story together. Or stop when you get to an exciting moment and ask your child what he thinks is going to happen next. It doesn't matter if his ending coincides with the author's. In fact, the more outrageous, the better.

You may not finish the tale, but so what? Your goal here is to have fun and be flexible. Besides, you can read another installment soap opera–style the next time. This approach has the additional benefit of helping a youngster think on his own, make choices, and enjoy your full attention.

3. *Read with your child rather than to her.* Encourage Emily's questions and comments. The process may be more important than the content. Even if she interrupts, she is relating to the story. Ask her why she has posed particular questions. Her answers will clue you into her thought processes.

STORYTELLING

This is one of the easiest ways to play with your children since it requires no special equipment and can be accomplished virtually anywhere at anytime—in the car, on the way to or from day care, at the market while you're pushing the cart down the aisle, at the service station waiting for the oil to be changed.

Storytelling is different from reading because it involves the recounting of a fable that you've created. You will find it easier to develop your fantasy world and help your children enrich their imaginations when you tell stories.

"Well, wait a minute," you might be thinking. "Stop right there. I'm an engineer. I know how to design jet engines, but I don't know the first thing about making up stories for kids."

Ah, but there you are wrong. You know lots of stories, maybe even thousands of them. For this activity, you rely on the events in your own life. Simply choose any experience you want to share and change the characters to animals.

Young children love to hear stories about their little furry friends. Bugs seem to go over well, too. Change your voice to suit the characters you've created, using animated, high squeaky tones for birds, mice, and caterpillars and deep rumbles for bears, tigers, and elephants. Kids can relate to these creatures and they become enraptured.

For example, if you want to instruct your young daughter about the dangers of taking on tasks for which she is not yet fully equipped, you can relate an experience you had as a child. Keeping in mind the animal proviso, transform yourself into a little mouse. Give him a name like Horace, and explain that since he was wearing his "Supermouse" cape he felt capable of any feat of strength. Horace wanted to carry a BIG piece of cheese despite his parents' objections. He, of course, couldn't handle the load. He dropped it into the river and the rest is, as they say, mouse history.

In concluding the story, you could say, "You know, a similar thing happened to me once, when I was about your age." Your daughter may be eager to know how you had messed up, so you can relate your own experience.

One father, Paul, described how, as a child, he had cut his finger while trying to whittle a piece of wood with a dull pen knife. Not knowing what to do about the gash, he left a trail of Mercurochrome splotches, cotton, Band-Aid wrappers, and blood behind him. What a mess!

Paul transformed this unfortunate incident into a tale of a young crocodile, Henry, who hurt himself while trying to fashion a crocodile house out of a piece of driftwood. His son's favorite stuffed animal was a toy crocodile.

You can use stories to teach your children moral lessons, but their impact will depend on your kids' ages. Preschoolers, for example, still don't have a strong sense of right or wrong. They learn from the consequences of what happens to them, *only*. But a story can be a "teachable moment." For example, Paul used his tale about the hurt crocodile to tell his son how to handle a cut finger in an emergency. On the other hand, you will feel most successful if you look upon storytelling as a way to create bonding with your kids. It's great fun.

Once you become involved in the spirit of storytelling, your own playfulness will take over. If you have difficulty or feel inhibited, it's helpful to write in a journal or just talk into a tape recorder. Besides, kids love tall tales—even if you're not "the best" at imaginative storytelling. And they love it even more if the story comes from you, for you are letting them into your life in a profound way.

PUPPETS

When you play with puppets, you and your kids express unresolved feelings and issues. You can use your children's stuffed animals or puppets to dramatize the stories you've created, especially if your kids are between the ages of two and seven (and still able to suspend their disbelief). As the puppeteer, you can imbue the toy with traits you value, such as cleanliness, teamwork, integrity, and candidness. Puppets can help you get your point of view across to your children without your sounding overly parental and authoritarian, and thus engendering your kids' resentment.

When your kids become puppeteers, they may guilelessly express their innermost feelings and perceptions. Children love puppets because they're so easy to control. You can create a dialogue of puppets to help air feelings and resolve issues between you. Puppet kisses are great.

Best of all, you don't even need equipment for puppet play. Like the father in the previous chapter, you can create your own puppets from table napkins and handkerchiefs. Old socks also work. You can even draw eyes, noses, and mouths on your (and your kids') fingers to create an instant family of puppets who act out small situation comedies derived from your family's experience. That kind of spontaneous puppet play can take place while waiting for your pizza to be baked or the movie to start.

ROUGHHOUSING

Roughhousing is a male form of play that occurs naturally and without any special equipment. It is an outgrowth of normal child development, a natural kind of physical contact that children engage in as they become more ambulatory. Toddlers who are crawling around will sooner or later crawl on top of you.

During this nonverbal interaction, gratification is immediate and instantaneous. You may be lying on the floor watching a football game and simply let your kids tumble and fall all over you. As long as you aren't doing two-and-a-half gainers with your youngsters, roughhousing provides a great opportunity to have lots of physical and emotional contact and just plain fun without any structure. In fact, this kind of play is entertaining and relaxing for parents and children alike and in some families continues through adolescence.

The physical and emotional contact that occurs during roughhousing is vital for bonding. All humans need physical touch. In fact, according to UCLA professor Susan Ludington-Hoe, newborn babies gain weight faster when they are exposed to regular rhythmic stroking. The touching that goes on during roughhousing is stimulating to your child. In addition, he connects to your body scent, the gurglings of your stomach, and the feel of his skin against yours. These all add to his sense of connectedness.

You may not realize that roughhousing also has an emotional component. During this kind of play you engage in lots of hugging and giggling and kissing with your kids. Roughhousing is an expression of your affection and in some families becomes a ritual.

Some staunch advocates of roughhousing even attribute better social skills to the rough-and-tumble activity. According to Rick Porter, founder of the Los Angeles Fatherhood Forum, director of the Rainbow River Child Care Centers in Los Angeles and Orange counties, and proponent of this kind of play, "Roughhousing is one way children learn that life is bumpy and that they will have to rely on their own determination to ride it out. The lesson isn't just physical, either. The kind of fortitude children get from roughhousing is the same chutzpah they'll have to muster when they're standing up for their rights or trying to assert a viewpoint in an executive boardroom."

The calm that follows a session of roughhousing is enjoyable, too. Your kids will relax and fall into you like a sack of potatoes lying on your chest. It's a wonderful way to release energy, but it needn't go on for hours. Depending on a child's age, five to fifteen minutes is appropriate. Use your best judgment. If you've stopped having fun, there's no point in continuing. Be sensitive to your and your children's comfort level.

If you want to roughhouse appropriately and safely, simply lie on the floor. You become a jungle gym for your kids and your nose, fingers, arms, and legs become play objects. You can also give a certain form to the play by saying to your child, "I'm a tree," or "I'm a snake." Then the roughhousing will lend itself to imaginative as well as physical play.

Here are some other safety tips that will enhance your game:

• Limit the time so that no one gets exhausted and keep to your limit.

• Roughhousing does not mean physically harming or hurting the other person. No pinching, biting, hair pulling, or kicking. Just fun.

• Remove shoes, belts, jewelry, or other objects that may inflict injury during the tussle.

• Be in the receiver position on the floor. Your kids should fall on you, but you should *not* fall on them.

• Indoors, roughhouse away from objects that you can tumble onto, break, or impale yourselves upon. The area should be padded or carpeted.

• Avoid linoleum, hardwood floors, ceramic tile, or concrete. The kitchen and bathroom are off limits.

• Outdoors, roughhouse on the grass. Give yourself enough space to allow your kids to fall on you or roll around. Keep away from prized flower beds, rosebushes, or other shrubbery.

• Grab your kids by their arms or torsos rather than by their fingers, which are easily twisted or bent.

• If you're holding your child, just hold him. We're not looking for full nelsons or arm- or headlocks.

• In the natural course of play, your kids will end up in any position, including upside down. Ask your daughter if she is okay many times during the play. Most likely, she will jump back on top of you after a breather.

• Stop when you're at the peak of your fun. You'll all want to get back to the game the next time you play. Or, at the very least, stop when your children want to. Respect that limit.

If, for whatever reason, someone gets hurt during the play, it's important to talk about how to improve roughhousing so your children will be eager to play again. It may mean trimming your fingernails or taking off your glasses. But just because your children experience some pokes and bumps doesn't make roughhousing bad. It's all part of the experience.

On the other hand, the potential for injury can be an issue for mothers because many women are unfamiliar with this kind of play and may become anxious when their husbands roughhouse. Yet dads report that their kids seemed more resilient toward bumps and falls after regular roughhousing play.

A word of caution: Roughhousing is clearly not for newborns or babies under one year of age. Lots of fathers enjoy rocking or spinning in space with their babies in their arms. Five- or six-month-olds giggle at feeling a sensation of gravity, and even younger babies benefit from the stimulation of their sense of movement. Dancing around with your baby is safe if you hold him close and support his head. But be careful. As Dr. Susan Ludington-Hoe and Susan Golant explain in *How to Have a Smarter Baby*, "Any movement that allows the head to move separately from the body before one year of age may contribute to bruised brain tissue." I've made some suggestions on suitable play with newborns in Chapter 7.

Finally, roughhousing teaches your children that although the world may be a jostling place, it is not necessarily unfriendly. When you walk down a busy street, you often get pushed and jostled. But the feeling is not necessarily that of danger. Rather, there is a certain excitement and comfort in seeing a street filled with people. Consider New Orleans during Mardi Gras. Now that's roughhousing on a rather grand, adult scale.

CLAY

Playing with clay helps to get you and your children involved in textures and smells. Clay figures provide a vehicle to explore your children's fantasy world: characters can be created, altered, and destroyed in an instant. Clay manipulation is also great for working off anger and frustration in the service of intimacy. When you pound and squeeze, you can all let off some steam.

Create imaginative, abstract shapes to get away from the compulsion to sculpt perfect forms. One father was able to let go of having to produce snails and dogs. Mark suddenly found himself capable of getting into more creative areas with his daughter. He watched in fascination as Staci fashioned hamburgers, pizzas, and grapes during clay play. Mark had never realized how interested she was in foods. Sometimes the two of them made animals, but rather than your standard horse or dog, they created magical beasts with fanciful bodies. Each added to the other's fantasy.

You can start your play simply by smelling, poking, pounding, and making sounds with the clay. Roll little clay balls and flatten them into pancakes. Coil snakes or worms into baskets. Then move into more whimsical play.

In fact, the making of objects can lead to imaginative games. If you've made a snake, for example, you can say, "The snake is looking for more snakes to make a snake family. Can you make a mama snake and baby snakes? What should we name them? And now the snake family is hungry; they're looking for food. Let's make snake food. What do snakes eat, anyway? How about their house? What kind of a house do you think our snake family lives in? Let's make one. Are the snakes happy today or sad? Why?"

As you become engaged in your activity, you'll find that communication occurs as the by-product of the play. You're creating the opportunity to learn about your children's imaginations and feelings.

A practical note: Clay has the tendency to become embedded in carpeting and upholstery. It's safest to do your sculpting on hard surfaces (such as the kitchen table or floor) covered with newspaper. Weather permitting, you can play with clay outside, where you won't have to worry about stray clay crumbs being ground into the linoleum.

CRAYONS AND MARKERS

Squiggling, smelling, breaking—you can use crayons with your children to foster imagination. Coloring books tend to limit the scope of fantasy play. Why not draw together on blank paper and make up stories to go along with your pictures? Again, this is a marvelous way for you and your kids to communicate meaningfully. You need not be an artist—far from it. Indeed, the *scribble game* and the *squiggle game* will help get you started.

During the scribble game you and your children can imagine that you have hung a big piece of paper in the air. Fantasizing that you're two or three years old (maybe one of you is!), close your eyes and scribble in the air with an outstretched finger. Make big imaginary circles or lines. Next, reverse the direction in which you are drawing. The goal of this exercise is to loosen up and experience your creative energy.

Usually after a few minutes of imaginary scribbling, you may begin giggling. It's as if the game reduces your inner tension about being an "artist" or creating a perfect drawing. You may be amazed at how relaxed you've become.

Next, get on the floor to do some real scribbling on paper. You only need a few crayons or markers to really get into it. After you've scribbled to your hearts' content, step back for a moment and evaluate your work. Your masterpieces may resemble something your toddler threw up that morning or, better yet, canvases painted by drip artist Jackson Pollock gone mad.

That's exactly the lead you should look for, because the next step is to examine the drawings and identify any common objects, animals, or toys that are lurking among the scribbles (in the same way you would visualize objects in cloud formations). Take a contrasting crayon or marker and highlight whatever object you can see: cars, wheels, letters. The fun is in having created something out of nothing, an activity that carries a marvelous sense of discovery.

The scribble game also provides an opportunity to observe what your kids see and how they think. In its own funny way, scribbling is a wonderful projective test—like an inkblot. You can look at a mass of tangled lines and see an ice cream cone, while your son may see flames shooting skyward from a wrecked airplane. While neither point of view is right or wrong, such disparities form the basis of some great conversations. "Gee," you may say, "what made you think about that?" It may be that the news report about a recent plane disaster had more of an impact on him than you'd realized. And that would be important for both of you to talk about.

Sometimes it's fun to make up stories combining elements and objects you find in your drawing: a ladder, a car, the letter *A,* a person, or a duck. This is also a wonderful way of making a connection.

The squiggle game is a variation of the scribble game. Make a squiggle and ask your kids to follow your lead. You may fill up whole pages together. Each time you make a squiggle, it increasingly resembles a real object. You each add on little pieces. Or you can take turns. Your children can make a squiggle and you turn it into something. Then you can make a squiggle and have them come up with an idea. Again, the idea is to create something out of nothing.

The squiggle game is enormously liberating: it's purely imaginative play at its best. You can't make mistakes because you start out with a mistake. The squiggle in and of itself doesn't mean anything. Believe it or not, that helps you deal with a traditional male struggle. When many men draw, they often get caught up in striving to make a perfect car or house. It's not that drawing a house isn't fun, but I am offering you another way of playing—one that has no preconceived expectations.

Playing with crayons and markers need not be limited to

designated times at home. Keep some supplies handy in the glove compartment of your car. Bring them along to pass the time meaningfully during plane and car trips or long waits at the doctor's office, airport, or restaurant.

BIKE RIDES

You may approach bike riding with a certain seriousness of purpose. It's good exercise and it gets you where you're headed faster than mere walking. But bike rides (with your child secured in a kiddie seat behind you or along side on his own tricycle or two-wheeler as he gets older) also provide excellent opportunities for interaction and even singing. The significance lies in what you talk about while en route as well as upon reaching your destination. As with the other activities, use your bike rides as an opportunity to interact.

CAR RIDES

Most of us spend a good portion of each day in the car and are not very happy about it. Sometimes we forget that there are all kinds of ways of getting from here to there and back. We can rush through our errands with a single-minded goal of getting to a destination, or we can use the process of driving to squeeze in fathering moments.

When your children are your passengers, you can use the time spent driving to and from school, Grandma's house, or day care for discussion, interaction, songs, and word games. In fact, you can even tell your children how much you love them during one of your car trips. You can compliment them on their growth or their progress in school or sports. In that way, you will be taking an everyday event and making an impact—it's a great way to seize the moment. And your children will remember and value these precious, relatively uninterrupted minutes spent with you.

SILLY DADDY

This is the most fun! Dads can be giggly, silly, fun-loving people. It's useful to know that your youngster's sense of humor depends on his stage of development. A toddler who is asserting his own identity will laugh when you mimic his habits. Your eighteen-month-old who is learning about how the world is ordered will giggle with delight if you pretend to suck his pacifier or bottle or if you wear his training pants on your head like a new and fancy hat. A two-year-old mastering language will enjoy nonsense syllables and nursery rhymes such as "The Itsy-Bitsy Spider" or "Hickory Dickory Dock." If your three-year-old is conquering toilet training, jokes involving bathroom functions will enthrall him. Between the ages of four and five, your youngsters will enjoy simple riddles and "knock-knock" jokes, as well as funny faces.

Silly daddy activities can also be physical. Play hide-and-seek or cavort as the goofy monster in the closet. Try monkey in the middle or have a dirty sock fight. Original, spontaneous games are some of the most joyful and rewarding moments of fatherhood. Laughing with your kids until everyone's sides hurt releases tension and stress. And it lets your children know that there's more to Dad than the grim-faced, square-shouldered man gritting his teeth and rushing off to work every morning.

School-Age Children

After about the age of six, children compete, strive to master skills, and eventually feel competent and confident. They become concerned about fair play and winning (see Chapter 7). While it is natural to engage in competitive play at this time, you may also continue and elaborate on the noncompetitive activities enjoyed earlier—take longer, more purposeful bike rides; read more complex books; draw more elaborate designs; have serious talks about economics, politics, or your feelings.

Involving your school-age kids in your hobbies and interests is another excellent opportunity to find the time for fathering. After all, if you're going to spend two precious hours of the weekend washing your car or building a deck, you might as well include your kids. While the teaching of skills may be valuable, that's not the point of this activity. Rather, you'll be sharing why you enjoy the hobby in the first place. Emphasize the pleasure you derive from polished chrome or perfectly parallel joists. Express satisfaction in doing what you love most. Direct your kids' attention to your emotional and esthetic responses to the activity. Not only will you engage them in your excitement, thereby sparking their own, but you'll also show them how you think and what you find important.

Sometimes kids can participate directly; on other occasions, they can engage in parallel activities. For example, you may find 1,000-piece jigsaw puzzles relaxing but be reluctant to include your seven-year-old because the puzzle is too difficult or you fear she'll inadvertently lose some pieces. Why not let her set up her own 100-piece puzzle next to yours? You can share your enthusiasms, frustrations, and triumphs and spend time together even though you're working on different designs.

The possibilities are limited only by your own interests. The following are suggestions for involving your school-age youngsters in noncompetitive activities that you may all enjoy.

PHOTOGRAPHY

If at all possible, buy your youngster an inexpensive box camera and slide film—preferable because it's cheaper to develop and you can print only the shots that aren't blurry. Or, for immediate gratification, get a simple instant camera. Encourage her to take pictures whenever you do—at family gatherings, birthday parties, sporting events, performances involving your other children, vacations, and excursions to the beach. Give advice on lighting and composition, but let her experiment and learn from mistakes. As she masters the technique, show her how a camera works and demonstrate f-stops, lenses, focusing, and settings on your own 35-millimeter version. If you have a darkroom, explain the chemicals and procedures and let her participate in developing her own pictures. While you both engage in photography, express your pleasure in designing a composition, seeing an image captured, taking nature shots, or waiting for the right moment and lighting for that perfect photo.

COLLECTING

Whether you enjoy collecting antiques or stamps, beer steins or baseball cards, you can include your kids in your passion. Take them to swap meets, art galleries, garage sales, stamp and coin shows, or other locales where collectors find treasure troves. Point out what makes certain objects valuable or desirable to help them understand your enthusiasm. Talk about varieties, colors, distinguishing differences. Explain how you decide to complete a series and why one object is more important than another. Get them started on their own collections; you'll spend time together poring over stamps or objets d'art.

COMPUTERS

Involve your kids in your favorite piece of electronic equipment. Show them how to boot up the computer. Explain the operating system and let them fiddle with the keys. Provide them with a typing and word processing tutor, and let them file notes, stories, jokes, and expressions of affection in their own "secret" mailboxes. If you have graphics software, let your kids create interesting designs. Their familiarity with the computer will serve them well in school. Of course, computer games are a natural, but the above noncompetitive activities will help your children learn about the other things the computer can do. Make it clear that you love how the computer allows you to accomplish difficult tasks with ease.

Sports

If you enjoy watching sports on TV, sit with your youngsters and explain to them the rules of the game and the plays as they unfold. Let them share your excitement and teach them to appreciate the tension between, say, the batter, the catcher, and the pitcher. This activity can be especially valuable if they're involved in team sports. You'll enjoy attending professional games together, but if that's impractical, watch the local high school team play. (To a seven-year-old T-ball enthusiast, adolescents may seem as professional as the pros!)

If you play tennis, badminton, handball, Ping-Pong, volleyball, or other ball and net sports, try to keep a rally going for as long as you can rather than playing for points (and winners or losers). If you must inject an element of competition, aim at beating your last round. If, for example, you and your son were able to hit the ball thirteen times before it landed out of bounds, next time try for fifteen. This has the dual advantage of sharpening your youngster's skills while building a feeling of cooperation and partnership.

Outdoor Activities

Enjoy hiking, rock climbing, fishing, and camping as a family. Teach your kids how to set up camp, start a camp fire, and recognize poison ivy and poison oak. Explain fire safety procedures and what to do if they become separated from you. Then go on a nature hunt together to identify flora and fauna. Involve them in gathering kindling and roasting wieners. Such activities help develop self-reliance. Campfire stories and songs are great fun, too. As you hike, express your love of nature: the scent of the pine forest, the wildflowers and animals, the wind whistling through the mountains, the panoramic views.

Some national parks have well-established summer campgrounds with concrete-floored cabins, beds and blankets, wood-burning stoves, showers, and mess halls. You need bring only a change of clothes, trail mix, sufficient water, and first-aid gear to enjoy the splendors of nature together.

If you're a skier, take your kids out on the slopes. Give them lessons (or hire an instructor) on the bunny runs. As they gain strength and confidence, ski together. Try cross-country skiing. It's great exercise and it gives you the opportunity to "hike" through miles of beautiful snow-covered countryside. Explain how you love the schussing of skis on fresh powder, the pristine whiteness of the slopes, the excitement of wind against your face as you speed down the mountainside, and that cup of hot chocolate when it's all over.

AQUATIC ACTIVITIES

In a pool or lake, you can teach your youngsters how to swim, dive for quarters and from the diving board, do the butterfly and backstroke, play "Marco Polo," and snorkel (in preparation for future trips to tropical waters). If your children know how to swim and you live close to an ocean, teach them to boogie board near the shore when you go swimming. You can even boogie board together. Here, too, it's important to convey safety rules, such as swimming near a lifeguard in safe tides and only going out with a buddy.

With appropriate safety gear and swimming skills, you can also include your kids in boating, jet skiing, water skiing, sailing, and other water-based pastimes.

As you play in the water, talk about your love and deep respect for the ocean and the quietness you find in scuba diving or snorkeling. Swimming is invigorating, and high diving is as close as you can come to flying.

CARS

Many men enjoy washing, waxing, or otherwise tinkering with their vehicles. If you're so inclined, teach your kids the mechanics of an internal combustion engine or engage them in a combined car wash–storytelling session. Why not have your kids wash their bikes while you polish your chrome? Make the activity enjoyable by telling jokes and riddles as you work.

If you're a car aficionado, ignite a similar love by taking your kids to car shows and car dealerships where you can all check out the new models. Share your fantasies and have your youngsters compare features advertised in glossy brochures. Antique car shows are also great, as are yearly gatherings of Mustang and Corvette owners.

Talk about the first time you got behind the wheel or what it was like to own your car. Describe the sights and sounds and mishaps you might have encountered while driving.

THE ARTS

If you sing, dance, play a musical instrument, sculpt, draw, or paint, explain your activities and teach your kids how to enjoy them, too. You can create art side by side, but be sure to withhold judgment. Let your youngsters express themselves in any way they want. Teach your youngsters songs and harmony for duets.

If you're more passive but no less enthusiastic in your involvement with the arts, simply take your children along to museums, art galleries, concerts, dance performances, and the like. Explain what you see in the paintings or talk about why certain music or dance makes you feel happy or sad. Your community may offer children's concerts and plays or child-oriented museum tours. Your kids might enjoy concerts that aren't too loud or rowdy. (It helps if you're familiar with the music first.)

When you introduce your youngsters to excellence, they learn models to emulate. Just bear in mind that their attention spans may be shorter than yours. Once they become restless, it's best to leave.

SCIENCE

An easy way to engage your kids in your love of science is to have them participate in gardening with you. While you're planting your summer garden, help them hoe their own row and sow seeds. Vegetables like carrots, zucchini, radishes, tomatoes, and sweet peas are relatively easy to grow. Zinnias, cosmos, and marigolds also sprout quickly. If you live in an apartment, use paper cups with holes punched in the bottom or flowerpots in a sunny window.

Your kids may perform experiments by withholding water, sun, or fertilizer from various plants. They can learn the principles of science by hypothesizing the outcome and then evaluating the result. Express your pleasure in watching your garden flourish and in reaping a bountiful harvest.

The care and feeding of pets can also be a fathering project. Show your youngsters how to brush the dog, feed the parakeet, or clean the fish tank. Point out how pets can be companions that help you feel wanted and loved. Talk about pets you owned as a child. Take regular trips to the pet store to observe tropical birds, lizards, and snakes. At an excursion to the zoo, compare household pets with the hyenas and tigers. Dealing with pets helps children accept responsibility and learn about life and death.

If you're interested in engineering, point out bridges, skyscrapers, dams, or other feats of engineering as you drive past them. Talk about the planning that goes into constructing these structures and the principles of physics that may apply. If you enjoy fixing electrical appliances, have your kids watch as you take them apart and reassemble them. In fact, make a mystery of it. ("I wonder why the mixer stopped working. Let's see if we can discovery what happened.") Talk about electromagnetic force, the motor, and electrical current. You might help your kids build battery-operated light switches and bells, a crystal radio, or a rudimentary motor. Explain how much you enjoy taking things apart and discovering how they work.

Visits to children's museums, aquariums, arboretums, observatories, museums of natural science, the Grand Canyon (and other geological formations), and museums of space exploration and industry are also marvelous opportunities to share your curiosity and love of science with your kids.

CONSTRUCTION PROJECTS

Some dads are consummate do-it-yourselfers. If you fall into that category, let your kids work alongside you. Depending on their age and dexterity, they can bring you tools, hammer in nails, measure and saw wood with a handsaw or power saw (with careful instruction, supervision, and assiduous use of safety gear), apply paint, help hang wallpaper, or, at the very least, hold the extension light. Whether you're building a bookcase or remodeling your home, you can get them busy with a simple doghouse made from leftover scraps of wood. Kids develop an enormous sense of pride and accomplishment when they've helped create something useful for the whole family. And the feeling is all the more powerful when they know they've worked on the project with you.

Adolescents

As your kids reach adolescence and move toward independence, their time with you shrinks. At this age they focus on their peer group and the forging of a separate identity. All is not lost, however. Often you can continue activities enjoyed prior to adolescence. Just remember to include your children's friends. When you take friends along to the amusement park or on camping trips or involve them in building projects, you let your adolescents know you're respectful of their moves toward independence and peer relationships. When they realize their friends are acceptable to you, they feel validated in their separate lives.

You'll also find your adolescents (especially a son) eager to beat you at sports and games. At this age, you might look upon your offspring as partners rather than competitors or apprentices. If they insist on competing and winning at all costs, allow them to win graciously and with praise based upon diligent effort and intensity of play. The torch has been passed to the next generation.

Competitive Play and Criticism

Since competition is so much a part of our culture, it's impossible to avoid these games with your kids. Yet the competitive spirit must be used wisely and in a focused way in order to benefit your children. Youngsters respond well to encouragement but shrink from criticism, just as adults do. When you make such statements as

- "You're not trying hard enough."
- "You're just lazy."
- "What's wrong with you, anyway?"
- "The other kids can do it. Why can't you?"

you undermine self-esteem and create distance between you. Moreover, your reproaches probably won't help your children's performance. If professional athletes place unreasonable demands on themselves, their performance actually suffers. Bringing this concept down to your children's level, your reprimands and judgment become internalized as self-criticism and self-doubt.

Men in our society have been taught that criticism equals caring. The reasoning goes something like this: "I love you enough to tell you when I think you're making a mistake. Who else will tell you the truth?" Certainly criticism can teach children to discriminate between what comes easily and where they can stand to improve, but kids' emergent egos are relatively delicate. Take it easy.

Besides, children grow at widely varying rates. Developmentally, your youngsters' coordination may be too immature to succeed at a given task, even if their agemates are already capable of it. Each child must be appreciated for his own strengths and talents.

How to Promote Supportive Competitive Play

To involve yourself with your child in competitive activities while being supportive, tell her that win or lose, she did her best. Emphasize the effort she exerted. Pay attention to how she went about playing rather than whether or not she won. And give her lots and lots of praise for what she did get right. You can say:

- "I know you gave it your best shot."
- "I saw you putting out a lot of effort."
- "You looked like you were really involved."
- "Even though it didn't go your way, you seemed to have fun."
- "Is there any area you'd like us to practice?"

How much fun is playing catch? Are you both laughing and smiling? Is this a happy time? Pay attention to your own style. If you find yourself angry or yelling a lot, you may want to pause for a moment to reevaluate and apologize. You're both supposed to be enjoying yourselves.

Also bear in mind that unless your daughter is an Olympic contender, there's always going to be someone "better" than her—just as there will always be someone with prettier clothes, higher test scores (in some subjects, at least), or a fancier car. That's how the world works. But simply because someone else is "better" doesn't invalidate her own achievements or her worth as a person. You can still praise her efforts to the skies, which will encourage her to strive even harder the next time.

In this chapter I have discussed ways for you and your children to share your worlds. This list is far from exhaustive. I wouldn't preclude the myriad of other talents and skills you bring to parenting, such as airplane piloting, filmmaking, writing, and cooking. These can also make for fun. By all means, use your imagination to come up with new activities. Moreover, books such as Susan Perry's *Playing Smart* and S. Adams Sullivan's *The Fathers Almanac* contain a myriad of inventive activities in which you and your kids can engage.

In the following chapter we will be moving from the security of home life out into the world at large. I will show you how you can find time for effective fathering even while you're working.

11

How to Incorporate Your Children into Your Daily Work

O N E hundred years ago, little Emily knew what her father did by looking out the window. She could see him plowing the field or shodding a horse. Work life and home life were closely related.

Today, youngsters often view the "office" and "plant" as distant and alien places. From my work with young children, I have found that their perceptions and descriptions of their fathers' workplaces are something out of a horror movie. These grim impressions are often the product of men's verbal expressions, such as "It's a jungle out there," "It was hell in the office today," "My boss is a slave driver," or "What a rat race."

Young children are very perceptive. They pick up subliminal messages when you grouse about your competitors, supervisor, or coworkers. In fact, kids' drawings of their fathers at work often show men with scary, distorted features, bulging eyes, and hair on end executed in the intense colors of black and red. Your own youngsters may be unaware that your work has many positive aspects. As we learned earlier, men's self-esteem is enhanced by their good feelings about work.

When you introduce your children to your work environment and include them in some way, your world outside the home becomes more familiar and less threatening and hostile to your family. At the very least, your youngsters become aware of where you spend so many hours each day—it's no longer a mystery. At best, they can see you as a competent adult in the world at large. Indeed, children can better accept your being gone at work when they conceptualize what you're doing in your absence.

Involving your kids is an excellent way to find time for fathering because by it you can enhance their attachment to you. It allows your children to spend time with you. In addition, it helps them develop positive images of you in your daytime environment that they can evoke and rely upon in your absence. As an extra benefit, incorporating your children in your work does not take a whole lot of extra time out of your busy day and can even improve work relationships by demonstrating to your coworkers that you have an emotionally rich life outside the work environment.

This chapter will support you in finding creative ways to include your children without feeling guilty about your career demands. I will show you how to bring your kids to your workplace or, if you can't, how to connect with them anyway.

Preschoolers

PHOTOGRAPHS

Something as simple as taking pictures can help bridge your work life and your home life for your children. As long as you're not working on some top secret, highly classified project for the Department of Defense, you can take photos of your workplace. (If you are in a restricted area, photos of the cafeteria and lobby or other public areas will work, too.) Have a coworker take a snapshot of you at your desk, on the assembly line, or at the construction site doing what you normally do. Take pictures of the people you frequently mention and of the cafeteria and the restrooms. (Kids are interested in bodily functions and where you take care of them!)

Sometimes it's fun to ham up the pictures. There's nothing wrong with your appearing silly or smiling. Besides, in that way, you communicate that work can be a pleasurable experience.

When you bring these photos home to your kids, you can say, "I just want to show you where I go each day." Your children can keep a scrapbook called *Where My Dad Works*. Depending on their ages, you can even add text explaining where you are and what you're doing. Your youngsters will refer to this scrapbook in your absence as a way of connecting to you.

Photographs can be used in other ways. For instance, keep your children's pictures with you at work (on your desk, in your wallet) as a constant reminder of your relationship with them. This helps to give you, your coworkers, and your clients the perspective that the work world is *not* your only world. There is much more to you—you're a loving father. You're showing that you're human, not just a boss or an employee.

In addition, you can leave pictures of you and your children together at home, at the day care center, or at nursery school as a reminder of your love for one another. Your youngsters can refer to them when they miss you. According to Dr. Susan Ludington-Hoe and Susan Golant, co-authors of *How to Have a Smarter Baby,* even week-old infants recognize their parents' smiling faces when those images are clearly represented in a black-and-white photo. Children are never too young to appreciate a picture.

You may have already bought a video camera to record your children's growing-up years. That's fine, but if you have the equipment (I'm not advocating that you run out and buy it this minute), you can also turn the camera on yourself and your work environment. Videotapes may ease your kids' fears about work and can help them to remain more connected to you during the week when you may see little of each other.

BRING YOUR WORK HOME

If at all possible, engage your kids in your work by bringing home a part of it that they can understand. If you're a designer or engineer, for example, show them mock-ups or blueprints; if you're a doctor, let them listen to their hearts with a stethoscope; if you're a salesperson, show them the products. Youngsters will understand your work and share your excitement and feelings of accomplishment when they can see the results of your labor.

FOUND OBJECTS

Sometimes your work is relatively intangible (your kids may have difficulty relating to a life insurance policy, for example), but you can still help them connect to you at work using found objects. When I was a teacher, I retrieved common classroom discards from the pile consigned to be thrown away. My kids cut and pasted faded pieces of construction paper that had adorned bulletin boards all year. These were no longer usable for my school purposes. I also salvaged leftover bits of yarn for art projects, used but perfectly serviceable watercolor paint kits that were to be thrown out, worn paintbrushes, and cast-off or discontinued textbooks and workbooks.

If you work in an office, you can recycle the end sheets torn from tracter-feed computer paper. These are great for art projects or for stuffing doll beds. Empty copier paper cartons can be put to a hundred uses, such as the construction of toy cars, make-believe kitchens, and pretend supermarket shelves. Larger boxes are great for hiding in or turning into a playhouse. My daughters even cherished little paper-clip boxes. They used them for storing beads, sequins, and glitter and for constructing furniture for their miniature dollhouse and its inhabitants. It doesn't take much to please young children.

If you're in construction, you can bring home bits of wood and nails for pounding, spools, and crates. Kids can play plumber with old pipes and faucets. You are only limited by your own imagination and concerns for your children's safety.

The point of this activity is not simply to cheaply augment your children's supply of play equipment, however.

When your preschoolers play with these cast-offs, they will associate them—the smell of the paper, the feel of the wood—with you and your work. In truth, these found objects are a great way to create and maintain contact with your kids while you're on the job. In the context of bonding, your recycling efforts can go beyond playing with toys. It may symbolize you in the world for your children. Recognize the value of objects not in and of themselves but for their value in your creating a relationship with your children.

AN ADVENTURE EXCURSION TO YOUR WORKPLACE

A trip to your workplace is important because it helps your children visualize and understand how your world is organized. When my daughters were young, I used to bring them to my classroom a day or two before the fall term began. This was a wonderful time for me that had little to do with the day-in, day-out chores of education such as grading papers, writing lesson plans, or controlling gang violence. Together we would organize the books and wall displays for the coming year. I introduced them to my coworkers while they were still relaxed and eager about the new school year. Best of all, my kids got to scribble all over the blackboard.

Even after I became a psychologist, my children continued to visit me in my office during breaks in my schedule or on the weekends. They played with my old psychological test kits (I never tested them) that contain blocks and pictures. They rocked in my desk chair and lay down on my couch. They always managed to find the crayons and paper, puppets, and stuffed animals that I keep for my youngest clients.

Of course, not every father will have a job or career that lends itself this readily to a child's world. But children are quite resourceful. I fondly remember occasions in which my dad took me to his cleaning plant on the weekends when the operation was shut down. I swung from the pipes as if they were part of a massive jungle gym expressly created for my delight while belting out Tarzan yells that I was certain had frightened away all of the wild beasts lurking behind the machinery.

Think about the fun parts of your work from your children's point of view. If you're a lawyer or are engaged in a similar office-centered business, you can let your kids sit behind your desk and twirl in your swivel chair. Or they can have great fun with your dictaphone, speeding up or slowing down their recorded voices. They may enjoy watching how the Xerox or fax machines work. And adding machines that spew forth rolls of tape are also big winners with kids, not to mention a blank screen on your computer. Even if you work in retail sales, you can let your kids play with a blank receipt book or straighten out stock. It makes them feel important.

If you are employed in a large factory, you may wish to take your children to one facet of the operation since the whole plant could be overwhelming or dangerous. One dad in our workshop assembled Camaros at a local Chevrolet plant. He brought his daughter to watch the cars get painted. Father and child then proceeded to the point at which the cars rolled off the assembly line. Tammy was very excited to see the finished product and to understand that her dad had something to do with it.

The following are general suggestions that will make the visit more successful.

1. *Prepare for the visit.* Before you actually bring your children into your workplace, you may want to do a bit of homework:

   • Check company policy about children visiting at work.
   • Find out if there are noise considerations or clothing restrictions; also, if hard hats or badges are required.
   • If your children can't visit during working hours, they might be able to share the lunch hour with you or could accompany you on your day off.
   • If visits are prohibited, difficult, or too dangerous, take a Sunday drive simply to show your children where you go when you leave for "work."
   • Prepare your children well, especially if they may encounter loud noises or dangerous machinery during the visit.
   • Make sure that they understand all safety rules in advance, and keep a watchful eye while they're on the premises.
   • If you're planning to get down to work, make sure that you have arranged for a ride home for your children.

2. *Be available during the visit.* Concrete markers make the work world real for children. Point out where you park your car, go to the bathroom, hang your clothes, eat, punch in, store your tools, and work.

   Introduce your children to your coworkers. If possible,

let them "help out." They can sit at a desk or "try" the cash register. If you're a teacher, allow your children to help out with bulletin boards or other school paraphernalia. Take photos of the visit showing you and your children at work, doing what you normally do.

Depending on your children's ages and attention span, try to keep the visit short and sweet—especially the first one. You don't want your kids to get bored or crabby. You'd like them to be eager to return.

3. *Follow up after the visit.* A recap with questions and answers is an essential part of your excursion. This provides a frame of reference for your children's understanding. Make sure you ask your youngsters what they think of your workplace. Review any comments your coworkers made about them. Ask your kids if they have any questions. Have them draw pictures of your workplace and then describe them. If a child is too young to write, he can dictate his impressions for you to write under his drawings. Discuss photos you might have taken and add these and the drawings to the *Where My Dad Works* scrapbook. In that way, you can amplify the experience so that it lasts many days and weeks.

School-Age Children

Children of seven and eight begin to have a more sophisticated understanding of your work environment. They are also eager to learn skills and accomplish tasks. You can use their natural enthusiasm and curiosity about your work to maintain and strengthen your bond.

Depending on your work situation (and there are constraints in every job), you might find ways to allow your school-age children to be your "helpers" at work from time to time. Simply tailor these suggestions to your own situation. Seven-year-olds can accomplish such basic tasks as counting coins, collating papers, stapling flyers, applying mailing labels, and packing envelopes. Older children can work the postage meter or organize and sort stock in a store. They can be especially helpful during inventory time. School-age kids love being involved in your work; it makes them feel important and "grown up."

You can bring your "helpers" to work once a month, say, on a Saturday morning when business is slow or you've come in to catch up. While I'm not advocating child labor, you should still compensate your children with an ice cream or a small hourly fee. Just be sure to respect your youngsters' shorter attention span. A couple of hours on the weekend or one morning during summer vacation may be all they can handle. Make arrangements for them to leave before they become bored or disruptive. And make sure to praise their efforts so they'll want to accompany you in the future.

Adolescents

If your adolescent is seeking an afternoon or summer job, you might see about her employment at your workplace. Developmentally, work is important at this age; on the job, adolescents are required to use increasingly complex interactive skills and develop autonomy. Your teen begins to enter the world of adults through work. It also benefits your relationship because you demonstrate your ever-increasing trust in her dependability. When you take your sixteen-year-old to work, she enjoys your recognition of her competence and importance.

Teenagers are capable of answering phones, working the cash register, scooping ice cream or making sandwiches, inspecting manufactured parts, typing and filing, waiting tables, selling merchandise, pumping gas, volunteering in hospitals, tutoring younger children, and a myriad of other service activities that don't require higher education.

You and your teen can develop camaraderie while working together. You can share your lunch hour or breaks. But perhaps more important, your adolescent can gain a sense of you from how your coworkers interact with her. "Your dad's a good guy. Isn't it great that he found a way to include you in work!" will show her that you're respected and valued.

One caveat here: Your teenager's focus is on independence. Be sure to allow her to make decisions on the job without your intervention. In addition, if she chooses not to work with you, don't insist. She is exercising her autonomy. Ask, "Is there any way I can help you find your own job?" Encourage her to follow through on leads. Help her prepare for interviews by rehearsing possible scenarios. If she's amenable, you can suggest possible attire and interview strategies. You can add, "I've had lots of experience in the world of work. Maybe you'll benefit from my successes and mistakes."

If You Work at Home

In the computer age, more and more people work at home and keep in touch with their office or clients through fax machines and modems. You may find yourself spending long hours working at home as an independent real estate broker, attorney, handyman, publicist, freelance writer, professor, student, or artist. One of the advantages of working at home is that you have the freedom to regulate your own schedule. One of the disadvantages is that you're always at work. The demarcation between family time and business is not so clearly drawn.

Even though your youngsters are around, you may need privacy to accomplish your work or, for safety reasons, may need them to keep away from your computer or other work-related tools. You may find it painful to be so close to your kids yet so unavailable. But no matter how you live, time and activities with your children are important and can be fitted in. You'll still want to build your kids into your work activities and explain what you do.

First, it's best to set up ground rules, including designated workspace areas that are either child-friendly or off limits. You can explain to your kids that they're free to visit when your door is open but that once you've closed it, they can't interrupt. If you're disturbed by family squabbles, the garage may be a more distant and suitable workplace for you.

Also keep in mind that you're actually on three-quarters time. Distractions and intrusions are bound to occur, so it's best to expect them and even plan for them. Let's face it, though, even in an office you're often interrupted by phone calls and coworkers' concerns. Some fathers use interactions with their children as planned breaks from more cerebral activities. You can make a 4 P.M. date with your son for fifteen minutes of shooting baskets or with your daughter for fifteen minutes at her tea party. Your kid will be delighted and you'll feel refreshed.

It's possible to allow your kids to share your workspace for limited periods of time. Cuddle your sleepy infant in a baby carrier while you work at your computer. Let your toddler play with blocks in his playpen next to your desk, where he'll be able to reassure himself of your presence from time to time. Your preschooler can paint quietly on the floor for ten minutes and your nine-year-old can work on her English composition, perhaps at her own little table set up in your room.

If your child is interested and capable of understanding, engage him in a discussion and demonstration of what you're busy working on. Show him how to send a fax message or push the button on the light meter for your camera equipment. Let him sit on your lap in front of the computer and do some "typing." He will find the opportunity to participate in your work stimulating and exciting.

All in all, getting your children involved in your work will help bring your family closer. But what if you're often called upon to travel for your business? Or what if you and your children must spend time apart due to divorce, vacations, boarding school, illnesses, or other circumstances? As we will see in the following chapter, there are ways to maintain contact with your kids and find time for fathering even if you must be separated.

12

Finding Time for Fathering When You Must Be Away

OUT of sight, out of mind? Hardly. If you must travel or be separated from your youngsters, I'm sure you think about your family back home. And your kids certainly spend lots of time thinking about you. But what are your children's thoughts like? Do they miss you terribly? Are they afraid you'll never return? Have they any idea where you've gone? The following story illustrates how sometimes we can't predict how our kids' minds work.

Many years ago, I took a business trip to Chicago when our younger daughter was only three years old. Aimee saw me board the plane when I departed, and she saw me exiting the plane when I arrived back home about seven days later. After discussing my trip with her for a bit, it became evident that for Aimee, my "going to Chicago" meant that I was flying around in an airplane for a week. Chicago was somewhere up in the air. Young children have a hard time understanding time and space.

Aimee's response points out how difficult it is for very young children to relate to their fathers' absences. This can be made even more trying if you're a salesperson with a territory to cover or if your work entails a lot of traveling.

Young children have no frame of reference. They don't fully understand conferences, conventions, hotel rooms, clients, or meetings. And some children imagine or fear that their dads evaporate in their absence.

One father in our group told of his son Tommy's difficulty in conceptualizing where he went when he left one weekend each month for Army Reserve duty. These were painful and frightening times for Tommy. He imagined that his father was actually fighting in a war during his absences since he was going to the "army."

The following suggestions will help you convey to your kids that even though you've had to be away on business or for other reasons, you're home with them in spirit. Some of the recommendations may involve taking a few minutes to consider your youngsters before you leave. This is time well spent. You'll also find that including your children in your work or play while you're out of town helps to assuage some of your guilt about being away. You're creating a link even when you're not there.

But whatever you do, don't limit yourself to my experience and imagination. Use the ideas that I share below as a springboard for your own creative solutions.

How to Include Your Children in Your Business Trips or Vacations

1. *Make preparations before you go.* Your electronic and photographic equipment can be handy tools once more. Record yourself reading favorite bedtime stories; your children can play the tapes in the evening or when they

miss you. If video equipment is available, a videotape of you reading to your children is also effective. If you don't have a video camera, you might ask your wife to take a picture of you reading while your children nestle up next to you. If your children tire of the same story, make new tapes at their request.

In a different vein, you may want to leave something of yours that's intimate or special, such as a T-shirt you've slept in or a handkerchief sprayed with your favorite aftershave. Children recognize and are comforted by articles of clothing naturally imbued with their parents' body scent. Such transitional objects help your youngsters feel secure on a very basic, perhaps even instinctual level. Indeed, newborn babies only several days old identify their parents from their scent.

2. *Keep contact while you're gone.* Record your trip. Take plenty of pictures of your hotel room, the scenery, the convention center, your colleagues or clients, or friends you've made on your vacation so your children understand where you've gone and that you haven't evaporated in your absence. You can even keep a journal of your trip to share with your family upon your return.

If at all possible, call daily. Even though the phone call may remind your children of your absence (and perhaps how much they miss you), it's important to make contact. In your conversation don't fail to tell your youngsters how much you love and miss them and when you'll call again. Note how many days remain before your return and mention some special event that may take place once you've returned. This will give them something to look forward to. If phoning is impossible, a daily postcard written during breakfast or before retiring will keep your youngsters informed of your progress and will maintain the connection. Your kids will look forward to hearing from you and can keep the cards in a scrapbook.

3. *Keep your shared hobby going with your school-age children* (see Chapter 10). If you're traveling abroad, you can pick up interesting postage stamps, coins, antique beer steins, or other collectibles, such as unusual shells, dolls dressed in ethnic attire, or local crafts and jewelry, to send home or share upon your return. Take pictures of the unfamiliar cars driven in the country, or of trains, boats, and planes. In some nations, bicycles, scooters, and mopeds are the transportation of choice and can be captured on film for future discussion. Send home photos, puzzles, or models of local monuments and architectural or artistic wonders, such as the Tower of London, the Eiffel Tower, a Shinto temple, or the Roman Forum. These can engender a discussion of history, geography, and politics. Leave a map showing what countries you'll be visiting on your trip.

If you're traveling within the United States, you can send or bring home models of the Statue of Liberty, the Washington Monument, or rockets from the Houston Space Center or Cape Canaveral. The Smithsonian in Washington, D.C., has a wealth of interesting science and industrial exhibits and may sell slides and models for you to share with your budding scientists. If you've got access to a modem, you can send messages to your youngsters' "secret" mailboxes.

Keep a log of local sporting events and purchase team sweatshirts or souvenirs for your little sports fans. If your youngsters enjoy skiing, write letters about how conditions in Vermont vary from those in Utah or California.

Children who love beach activities may be interested to hear how the Atlantic differs from the Pacific. Bring home shells and stones worn by the surf.

Take pictures to share with a budding photographer and explain how the quality of exterior light differs at various latitudes. If you've had an opportunity to visit museums or theatrical/musical events, send home catalogs, posters, photos, T-shirts, tape recordings, programs, or other memorabilia to your young painter, singer, dancer, or thespian.

4. *Recap the trip when you return.* Even if you're a frequent traveler, spend some time talking about the trip with your children. Each absence is unique to them. Share your adventures through the photos, souvenirs, and journal entries. Help them assemble a scrapbook of your trips. In some families, the day of Dad's return is a big celebration in which the wonders of the world slowly emerge from a battered suitcase.

By the same token, spend equal time hearing from your youngsters how they spent the week without you. Listen as they relate successes in math and difficulties in social studies. Share with them their excitement in scoring a goal at soccer and their frustration in arguing with friends. Encourage them to show you schoolwork or play the new piece they mastered at the piano.

5. *Help your youngsters deal with their feelings about your absence.* Use the experience to enrich your relationship with your kids by talking about everyone's emotional response to your absence. Share your feelings: tell your children about when you thought of them the most and how difficult it was for you to be away from the family or to miss an important milestone. Be open to hearing their

responses. Discuss missing one another. Validate your youngsters' emotions (by saying, "It must have been hard for you," or "You must have been lonely") and seek ways to make future absences easier for all to bear. Maybe it would be more effective to call in the morning rather than at bedtime. Maybe your kids became bored with one story; next time, tape four.

You may find so much openness difficult. Some dads experience troubling emotions at this transition time. They may resent that family life goes on just fine without them. They feel left out and, consequently, withdraw. Others suffer from guilt at having missed important occasions or even the ordinariness of everyday routines. In any case, they may have a hard time dealing with their feelings. They may gloss over their emotions and act as if they hadn't left at all. These responses are counterproductive. They shorten the time that can be spent interacting with the family.

While this stoic attitude may send the message that men are "tough," it does little to help children deal with feelings of abandonment. So, rather than defending against their emotions (by ignoring them or responding angrily to them) as a way to allay your own resentment or guilt, work with the experience in order to reintegrate yourself into the family. Address your children's feelings directly. Ask such questions as:

- How did you feel about my going away?
- Did you miss me?
- Did you feel sad?
- Did you feel frightened?
- Were you angry that I was gone?

- How do you feel now that I'm home?
- What can we do now that would feel special to you?

You can expect your children to feel sad or angry about your absence. Most kids do. After all, they love you and want you around. It's important for your youngsters to get their feelings off their chests, but it's equally important for you to tolerate their emotions, not deflect or negate them. If your children are angry at you, it's best to validate them by saying, "I know this was hard for you. You're sounding angry and you're entitled to feel that way. You don't like it when I'm gone."

To this, a child may add, "Yeah! I'm mad. I missed you. And you missed the home run I hit in baseball this week! Johnny's dad was there! Why weren't you?"

Again, you can validate feelings and let your children know that it's okay for them to express anger verbally. It is hard for you to be gone and none of the above activities can substitute for your presence. They are, in truth, the best you can do under difficult circumstances.

If a child doesn't express his hurt feelings, however, he may act out his anger in more negative or destructive ways (such as fighting with siblings, misbehaving at school, sulking, breaking a valuable possession, or regressing) in an attempt to gain your attention. When you allow a child to express his emotions freely within the context of your questions, he can release himself from their grasp and be better able to get on with having fun with you now that you're home.

What Your Children Can Do in Your Absence

There are many ways that your youngsters can stay connected to you during your travel. Leave behind notebooks or pad so that your kids may keep daily journals of their experiences and feelings while you're gone. If they are too young to write, they may draw pictures of activities or feelings or tape record their feelings. After your return, look at the journals (or listen to the tapes) together as a way of sharing. Try exchanging journals. Invite them to talk about how they felt while making the drawings.

Children can also record imaginary letters to you whenever they miss you or have some news to share. Replay and discuss the tapes upon your return. If they're old enough, of course, they can write to you. Help them understand that it may take several days for the mail to reach you and for you to respond to their concerns. Or they can communicate to you via the computer.

Your youngsters should also send along with you any important objects of theirs: a stuffed animal, a picture, a blanket or toy that will be in your safekeeping during your trip. Your kids can record a favorite song for you to play on your Walkman as a reminder of their importance to you. This will act as a reminder for you and will help them to feel that they are connected to you despite the miles that separate you.

Ask your wife to make a ritual of marking off the days on a calendar each evening when you call. This will help your youngsters visualize more concretely how many days remain until your return. Somehow it makes the time go faster. Once they're old enough, of course, they can do it themselves.

When Your Kids Have Gone to Camp or Boarding School

Treat situations in which your kids are absent much as you would if you were traveling. Before they leave, spend time talking about how much you're going to miss each other. Most likely, they'll be caught up in organized activities once they get to school or camp, but they'll still be thrilled to hear from you regularly by phone, letter, and tape (if they have a recorder). You'll enjoy it, too. When our kids were away, we needed those phone and mail connections as much as they did! The house felt empty without them.

Photos are great for keeping kids posted on changes at home. If it's permitted, send care packages of cookies, magazines, or comics you know they'll enjoy. Transitional objects are also important at this time, since they provide a reminder of love and security in an unfamiliar surrounding. When your kids return, it's important to talk about how much you've missed them and to marvel at how they've grown in the interim.

How to Stay Connected After a Divorce

Divorces and custody agreements are as unique as the people who must cope with them. Depending on the tenor of your divorce and your current relationship with your ex-wife, the logistics of spending time with your children may be more or less difficult: you may share custody, alternate weekends and Wednesday nights, take the kids for two months during the summer, or any other permutation of visitation rights.

Despite the difficulties, under most circumstances divorced mothers know that their kids are better off having some relationship with the fathers. Men provide a role model that women simply cannot duplicate. Clearly, you'll want to give your kids your full attention when it's your turn to parent, using all of the suggestions outlined in this book. But, by applying the recommendations in this chapter, you can also be with your kids in spirit, if not in body, during the times you're apart. For example, you can:

1. *Use audio and videotapes to keep in contact.* Record the fun you've had together so your children can listen to or watch tapes when you're not there.
2. *Tape stories.* Mail or drop these off to your children every week, along with the book you've read from so they can follow along. For a school-age child, tape seven chapters (one per night) of a book such as *Treasure Island* or *The Swiss Family Robinson,* taking breaks after each chapter to wish your youngsters pleasant dreams. Send the next seven chapters the following week.

3. *Introduce your kids to your work.* Have your coworkers take photos of you at work. Put together a scrapbook.

4. *Use television.* Agree to watch a favorite TV show and call each other to chat about it afterwards.

5. *Exchange transitional objects.* Give your children a well-worn sweatshirt or T-shirt and keep one of their favorite toys or stuffed animals.

6. *Carry on shared hobbies at a distance.* Mail or drop off interesting stamps, baseball cards, model airplanes, or other hobby-related objects.

7. *Exchange letters.* In the absence of videotapes, letters are a fine way to communicate. Send plenty of photos and ask for pictures in return.

8. *Schoolwork.* Ask your ex-wife or youngsters to send copies of the children's schoolwork and reports so that you may keep up with their intellectual growth. Return these to your children with words of praise about accomplishments and encouragement for how hard they're working.

9. *Subscriptions.* Shared magazine subscriptions, say, to *Motor Trends* for your young car buff or *Rolling Stone* for your rock fan, will help maintain a connection and give you subjects to talk about.

10. *Use pets.* Favorite pets can remind your children of you and the love you share.

11. *Deal with your emotions.* While you won't want to burden your youngsters with the Sturm und Drang of your divorce, you can certainly share with them how much you miss them now that you're no longer living together on a daily basis. Give them the opportunity to share their feelings, too. You'll all be ready to have fun when you've cleared the air.

Postscript

Over many years a gentle revolution has unfolded. Men have become more sensitive and emotional. They are genuinely listening to their wives and making themselves more available to their families. Yet two other images persist, each with important and moving implications.

The first dates to 1984 when the men's movement sociologist and leader Warren Farrell addressed the first Los Angeles Fatherhood Forum about what fathers can learn from their children. We in the audience were somewhat confused when he broached this topic. We understood how children could learn from fathers, but this reversal of the "natural" order seemed disorienting.

Dr. Farrell invited his stepdaughter up to the stage before this group of committed professionals. In a measured way, he asked her if she would show him how to execute a gymnastics routine that she had perfected. The twelve-year-old's excitement and pride as she "spotted" Farrell was almost palpable, as was this dad's awkward vulnerability as he learned the four movements. The audience twisted and strained with him.

When Farrell had achieved a modicum of proficiency, we

cheered wildly. And then we got it: this concrete example of a father learning from his child excited us. Inviting that possibility into our lives was thrilling and available at any level, from feeling mud between our toes to understanding complex computer technology. Our children have skills that we ignore or take for granted.

Paradoxically, the more you become involved in your daughter's reality, the more you can appreciate how different she is from you. If you approach your involvement with a sense of curiosity, you can learn how she thinks and that she has her own perspective about the world. You see her as a unique individual. When you allow your child to be your teacher, you reexperience some of the faltering steps in the tremendous struggle to achieve adulthood. You truly appreciate her progress and determination. You become more patient and more respectful. And also, paradoxically, your respect for her allows you both to grow close.

The second image I owe to Nancy, a member of a support group of ten to twelve single mothers. The women wished to attend a Finding Time for Fathering workshop. However, my workshops are usually exclusively male. Men need a forum in which they can speak freely, and for one reason or another (especially if role expectations intervene), that doesn't happen when women are around.

Nancy understood, yet she and her friends didn't know where to turn for help. "We realized that because of divorce, separation, or individual circumstances, something was missing in our homes besides fathers. Yet we can't put our finger on it," she explained. "I was hoping that you could help us identify that missing element." Nancy's was the first request of that sort that I had gotten, and so it occurred to me that I'd love to meet with her and the other women. However, I chose a different setting.

Our special workshop took place in an unused elementary school classroom. About ten women attended, all accompanied by their toddlers. I went through my routine workshop agenda: I spoke of men's impact on child development, sex role identification, and intellectual growth. That was all fine. But when I got to the section on how fathers nurture their children differently, bringing up roughhousing, several women immediately broke in. "Hold on. What are you talking about?"

"Roughhousing," I replied, matter-of-factly.

Blank stares. Everyone knew what the word meant, but none of the women could see its value when it came to bonding or to just plain fun. To them, roughhousing was potentially dangerous and rather pointless. I invited these mothers to push aside the furniture, get down on the floor with their toddlers right then and there, and roughhouse. The resulting squeals of laughter and delight made it seem as if the whole room had just given a collective sigh of relief. In that moment we captured a sense of appreciation for what fathers have to offer their children.

These two images have sustained me: the ability of fathers to let go of their roles as experts or authority figures, and the ability of mothers to recognize and appreciate fathers' unique contributions to the life of the family. What a wonderful world it would be if we could all break out of such preconceived notions. How much more common those special moments would become when people recognize others as just like themselves, all struggling to do what's best for children and families.

Bibliography and Suggested Reading

Abelin, E. L. "The role of father in the separation-individuation phase." In *Separation-Individuation: Essays in Honor of Margaret S. Mahler,* ed. J. V. McDevitt and C. F. Settlage. New York: International Universities Press, 1971.

Ainsworth, Mary D. Salter. "Attachments Beyond Infancy." *American Psychologist* 44 (1989): 709–716.

Azrin, Nathan H., and Richard M. Foxx. *Toilet Training in Less Than a Day.* New York: Simon & Schuster, 1974.

Barnett, R.C., and G. K. Baruch, "Determinants of fathers' participation in family work." *Journal of Marriage and the Family* 49 (1987): 29–40.

Baumrind, D. "Socialization and instrumental competence in young children." *Young Children* 26 (1970): 104–119.

———. "Social determinants of personal agency." Paper presented at biennial meeting of the Society for Research on Child Development, New Orleans, March 1977.

Bem, S. L. "Gender schema theory and its implications for child development: Raising gender-aschematic children in a gender-schematic society." *Signs* 8 (1983): 598–616.

Bennett, Susan M. "Family environment for sexual learning as a function of fathers' involvement in family work and discipline." *Adolescence* 19 (1984): 609–627.

Berman, P. W. "Are women more responsive than men to the young? A review of developmental and situational variables." *Psychological Bulletin* 88 (1980): 669–695.

Berman, P., L. Monda, and R. H. Myerscough. "Sex differences in young children's response to an infant: An observation within a day-care setting." *Child Development* 48 (1977): 1071–1077.

Biller, H. B. "The father and sex role development." In *The Role of the Father in Child Development,* 2d ed., ed. Michael E. Lamb. New York: John Wiley, 1981, 319–358.

Biller, H. and D. Meredith. *Father Power.* New York: Anchor Books, 1975.

Blackman, Anne, Elizabeth Taylor, and James Willwerth. "The road to equality." *Time* 136 (Fall 1990) 12–14.

Blanchard, Robert W., and Henry B. Biller. "Father availability and academic performance among third-grade boys." *Child Development* 4 (1971): 301–305.

Bloom-Feshbach, J. "Historical perspectives on the father's role." In *The Role of the Father in Child Development* 2nd ed., ed. Michael E. Lamb. New York: John Wiley, 1981, 71–112.

Bonker, Dawn. "Kids join a fray for all." *Orange County Register,* 27 July 1989.

Bowlby, J. *Attachment and Loss.* New York: Basic Books, 1969.

Bozett, F. W. "Male development and fathering throughout the life cycle." *American Behavioral Scientist* 29 (1985): 41–54.

Brazelton, T. B. *The Family.* Paper presented at Symposium, The Family, Philadelphia, November 1974.

Burns, Alyson L., G. Mitchell, and Stephanie Obradovich. "Of sex roles and strollers: male attention to toddlers at the zoo." *Sex Roles* 20 (1989): 309–315.

Canter, L., with Marlene Canter. *Assertive Discipline.* Los Angeles: Canter and Associates, 1976.

Clarke-Stewart, K. Alison. "The father's contribution to children's cognitive and social development in early childhood."

In *The Father-Infant Relationship: Observational Studies in the Family Setting,* ed. Frank A. Pederson. New York: Praeger, 1980.

Coleman, A., and L. Coleman. *Earth Father/Sky Father: The Changing Concept of Fatherhood.* Englewood Cliffs, N.J.: Prentice Hall, 1986.

Dickman, D. L. "The father/daughter bond." *Medical Aspects of Human Sexuality* 20 (1986): 80–84.

Emihovich, Catherine, E. I. Gaier, and N. C. Cronin. "Sex-role expectation changes by fathers for their sons." *Sex Roles* 11 (1984): 861–868.

Engel, Beverly. *The Right to Innocence: Healing the Trauma of Childhood Sexual Abuse.* Los Angeles: Jeremy Tarcher, 1989.

Erikson, Erik. *Identity: Youth and Crisis.* New York: W. W. Norton, 1968.

Evans, O. "400 ex-babies listen to Dr. Spock raptly." *New York Times,* 20 April 1989.

Ferber, Richard. *Solve Your Child's Sleep Problems.* New York: Simon & Schuster, 1985.

Field, T. "Interaction behaviors of primary versus secondary caretaker fathers." *Developmental Psychology* 14 (1978): 183–184.

Finkelhor, D. *The Sexual Climate in Families.* Paper presented at the meeting of the Society for the Scientific Study of Sex, Dallas, November 1980.

Fleming, D., with L. Balahoutis. *How to Stop the Battle with Your Child.* West Covina, Calif.: Don Fleming Seminars Publishing Co., 1982.

Fogel, A., G. F. Melson, and J. Mistry. "Conceptualizing the determinants of nurturance: A reassessment of sex differences." In *Origins of Nurturance: Developmental, Biological and Cultural Perspectives in Caregiving,* ed. Alan Fogel and Gail F. Melson. Hillsdale, N.J.: Lawrence Erlbaum Associates, 1986.

Frodi, A., and M. E. Lamb. "Sex differences in responsiveness to infants: A developmental study of psychophysiological and behavioral responses." *Child Development* 49 (1978): 1182–1188.

Furman, R.A. "The father-child relationship." In *What Nursery School Teachers Ask Us About: Psychoanalytic consultations in pre-schools,* ed. Erna Furman. Emotions and Behavior Monographs, no. 5. Madison, Conn.: International Universities Press, 1986.

Golant, M. C. *The Effect of Group Counseling on Locus of Control with Pregnant Teenagers.* Ph.D. Diss. University of Southern California. 1980.

Golant, M., and S. Golant. *Disciplining Your Preschooler and Feeling Good about It.* Los Angeles: Lowell House, 1989.

Golant, Susan. *The Joys and Challenges of Raising a Gifted Child.* New York: Prentice-Hall Press, 1991.

Golant, Susan K., and Mitch Golant. *Kindergarten: It Isn't What It Used to Be.* Los Angeles: Lowell House, 1990.

Goleman, Daniel. "Sensing silent cues emerges as key skill." *New York Times,* 10 October 1989.

———. "Studies on development of empathy challenge some old assumption." *New York Times,* 12 July 1990.

Goodenough, E.W. "Interest in persons as an aspect of sex difference in the early years." *Genetic Psychology Monographs,* 1957, 55:287–323.

Gottfried, A. E., A. W. Gottfried, and K. Bathurst. "Maternal employment, family environment, and children's development: Infancy through the school years." In *Maternal Employment and Children's Development,* ed. A. E. Gottfried and A. W. Gottfried. New York: Plenum, 1988, 11–51.

Greenberg, M., and N. Morris. "Engrossment: The newborn's impact upon the father." *American Journal of Orthopsychiatry* 44 (1974): 502–531.

Grief, Geoffrey L., and Cynthia Bailey. "Where are the fathers in social work literature?" *Families in Society* 7 (1990): 88–92.

Grossman, Frances K., William S. Pollack, and Ellen Golding. "Fathers and children: Predicting the quality and quantity of fathering." *Developmental Psychology* 24 (1988): 82–91.

Grossman, Frances K., William S. Pollack, Ellen Golding, and Nicolina M. Fedele. "Affiliation and autonomy in the Transition to Parenthood." *Family Relations* 36 (1987): 263–269.

Hite, Shere. *The Hite Report on Male Sexuality.* New York: Knopf, 1981.

Hochschild, Arlie, with Anne Machung. *The Second Shift: Working Parents and the Revolution at Home.* New York: Viking, 1989.

Hoffman, L. W. "Effects of maternal employment in the two-parent family." *American Psychologist* 44 (1989): 283–292.

Jacklin, Carol Nagy. "Female and male: Issues of gender." *American Psychologist* 44 (1989): 127–133.

Jacklin, Carol Nagy, and Eleanor E. Maccoby. "Social behavior at 33 months in same-sex and mixed-sex dyads." *Child Development* 49 (1978): 576–569.

Jolly, A. *The Evolution of Primate Behavior.* New York: Macmillan, 1972.

Jones, R. A., C. Hendrick, and Y. M. Epstein. *Introduction to Social Psychology.* Sunderland, Mass: Sinauer Associates, 1979.

Kantrowitz, B. "Advocating a 'mommy track.' " *Newsweek,* 13 March 1989, 45.

Kantrowitz, Barbara, and Pat Wingert. "How kids learn." *Newsweek,* 17 April 1989, 50–57.

Kessler, R. C., and J. A. McRae, Jr. "The effects of wives' employment on the mental health of married men and women." *American Psychological Review* 47 (1982): 216–227.

Kohlberg, Lawrence. "Stage and sequence: The cognitive developmental approach to socialization." In *Handbook of Socialization Theory and Research,* ed. D. A. Goslin. Chicago: Rand McNally, 1969.

———. "Moral stages and moralization: The cognitive-developmental approach to socialization." In *Moral Development and Behavior: Theory, Research, and Social Issues,* ed. T. Lickona. New York: Holt, Rinehart and Winston, 1976.

Krymko-Bleton, I. "Prenatal problems for future fathers." In *Pre-*

natal and Perinatal Psychology and Medicine: Encounter With the Unborn, ed. Peter Fedor-Frybergh and M.L. Vanessa Vogel. Park Ridge, N.J.: Parthenon Publishing, 1988, 123–128.

Kurshan, N. *Raising Your Child to Be a Mensch.* New York: Ballantine, 1989.

Kutner, Lawrence. "Parent and child: Respecting the closed door, and teaching respect for it." *New York Times,* 7 September 1989.

Lamb, M. E. "The development of parent-infant attachments in the first two years of life." In *The Father-Infant Relationship,* ed. Frank A. Pedersen. New York: Praeger, 1980.

———. "Fathers and child development: An integrative overview." In *The Role of the Father in Child Development* 2d. ed., ed. Michael E. Lamb. New York: John Wiley, 1981, 1–70.

———. "The changing roles of fathers." In *The Father's Role: Applied Perspectives,* ed. Michael E. Lamb. New York: John Wiley & Sons, 1986, 3–27.

Lamb, M. E., J. H. Pleck, and J. A. Levine. "Effects of paternal involvement on fathers and mothers." *Marriage and Family Review* 9 (1986): 67–83.

Levant, Ronald, and John Kelly. *Between Father and Child.* New York: Viking, 1989.

Lewin, T. "View on career women sets off a furor." *New York Times,* 8 March 1989.

Lewis, R. A. "Men's changing roles in marriage and the family." *Marriage and Family Review* 9 (1986): 1–10.

Ludington-Hoe, S., and S. Golant. *How to Have a Smarter Baby.* New York: Bantam, 1986.

Mabry, Marcus. "On Madison Avenue, Daddy sells best." *Newsweek,* 12 November 1990, 54.

Maccoby, Eleanor E. "Gender and relationships: A developmental account," *American Psychologist* 45 (1990): 513–520.

Maccoby, Eleanor E., and Carol Nagy Jacklin. "Gender segregation in childhood." In *Advances in Child Development and Behavior* vol. 20, ed. H. W. Reese. New York: Academic Press, 1987, 239–288.

McEnroe, Colin. "There's nothing like an extra man about the house." *San Jose Mercury News,* 27 October 1990.

McLoyd, V. C. "Socialization and development in a changing economy: The effects of paternal job and income loss on children." *American Psychologist* 44 (1989): 293–302.

Minsky, T. "Advice and comfort for the working mother." *Esquire* 101 (June, 1984).

Nickel, H. "The role of father in care-giving and in the development of the infant: An empirical study on the impact of prenatal courses on expectant fathers." In *Prenatal and Perinatal Psychology and Medicine: Encounter with the Unborn,* ed. Peter Fedor-Frybergh and M.L. Vanessa Vogel. Park Ridge, N.J.: Parthenon Publishing, 1988, 101–121.

Ninio, Anat, and Nurith Rinott. "Fathers' Involvement in the care of their infants and their attributions of cognitive competence to infants." *Child Development* 59 (1988): 652–663.

"Opinions about motherhood: a Gallup/Levi's maternity wear national poll," San Francisco: Levi Strauss and Co., September, 1983.

Osherson, Samuel. *Finding Our Fathers: How a Man's Life is Shaped by His Relationship with His Father.* New York: Fawcett Columbine, 1986.

Parke, R. D. "Perspectives on father-infant interaction." In *The Handbook of Infant Development,* ed. J. D. Osofsky. New York: Wiley, 1979.

Parke, R. D., and Douglas B. Sawin. "Fathering: It's a major role." *Psychology Today* 11 (1977): 109–112.

Perry, Susan K. *Playing Smart: A Parent's Guide to Enriching, Offbeat Learning Activities.* Minneapolis: Free Spirit Publishing, Inc., 1990.

Pleck, J., M. Lamb, and J. Levine. "Epilog: Facilitating future change in men's family roles." *Marriage and Family Review* 9 (1986): 11–16.

Radin, N. "Father-child interaction and the intellectual functioning of four-year-old boys." *Developmental Psychology* 6 (1972): 353–361.

———. "The role of the father in cognitive, academic, and intellectual development." In *The Role of the Father in Child Development* 2d. ed., ed. Michael E. Lamb. New York: John Wiley, 1981, 379–427.

———. "Childrearing fathers in intact families: An exploration of some antecedents and consequences." *Merrill-Palmer Quarterly* 27 (1981): 489–514.

Radin, N., and R. Goldsmith. "Caregiving fathers of preschoolers: Four years later." *Merrill-Palmer Quarterly* 31 (1985): 375–383.

Radin, N., and Russell, G. "Increased father participation and child development outcomes." In *Fatherhood and Family Policy*, ed. M. Lamb and A. Sagi. Hillsdale, N.J.: Lawrence Erlbaum Associates, 1983.

Roberts, E. J., D. Kline, and J. Gagnon. *Family Life and Sexual Learning: A Study of the Roles of Parents in the Sexual Learning of Children.* Cambridge, Mass.: Population Education, 1978.

Roggman, Lori A., and J. Craig Peery. "Parent-infant social play in brief encounters: Early gender differences." *Child Study Journal* 19 (1989): 65–79.

Rotundo, E. A. "American fatherhood: A historical perspective." *American Behavioral Scientist* 29 (1985): 7–25.

Russell, Alan, and Graeme Russell. "Warmth in mother-child and father-child relationships in middle childhood." *British Journal of Development Psychology* 7 (1989): 219–235.

Russell, G. *The Changing Role of Fathers.* St. Lucia, Queensland: University of Queensland Press, 1982.

Russell, G., and N. Radin. "Increased paternal participation: The fathers' perspective." In *Fatherhood and Family Policy*, ed. M. E.

Lamb and A. Sagi. Hillsdale, N.J.: Lawrence Erlbaum Associates, 1983, 191–218.

Sgroi, Suzanne, M. *Handbook of Clinical Intervention in Child Sexual Abuse.* Lexington, Mass.: Lexington Books, 1982.

Shapiro, J. L. "The expectant father." *Psychology Today* (January, 1987): 36–42.

Shedler, Jonathan, and Jack Block. "Adolescent drug use and psychological health: A longitudinal inquiry." *American Psychologist* 45 (1990): 612–630.

Siegal, Michael. "Are sons and daughters treated more differently by fathers than by mothers?" *Developmental Review* 7 (1987): 183–209.

Silverstein, Louise B. "Transforming the debate about child care and maternal employment." *American Psychologist* 46 (1991): 1025–1032.

Smuts, B. B. "Dynamics of 'special relationships' between adult male and female olive baboons." In *Primate Social Relationships,* ed. R. A. Hinde. Oxford, England, 1983.

Solomon, Neil. "Coping with the earthquake anxiety." *Los Angeles Times,* 25 October 1989.

Spieler, S. "Preoedipal girls need fathers." *Psychoanalytic Review* 71 (1984): 69–80.

Steinbrook, Robert. "Children's erratic eating habits seen as normal." *Los Angeles Times,* 25 January 1991.

Stern, Zelda. "Sleepless nights." *American Baby* (April 1986): 62–64.

Stewart, A. J., et al. "Adaptation to life changes in children and adults: Cross-sectional studies." *Journal of Personality and Social Psychology* 42 (1982): 1278.

Stewart, R., and R. Marvin. "Sibling relations: The role of conceptual perspective-taking in the ontogeny of sibling caregiving." *Child Development* 55 (1984): 1322–1332.

Sullivan, S. Adams. *The Fathers Almanac,* New York: Doubleday, 1980.

Suomi, S. J. "Adult male-infant interactions among monkeys living in nuclear families." *Child Development* 48 (1977): 1255–1270.

Thomas, Cal. "Must adolescence submit to the chain saw of sex education in the public schools?" *Los Angeles Times,* 27 April 1989.

Trotter, R. J. "The play's the thing." *Psychology Today* (January 1987): 27–33.

Turner, Jeffrey S., and Donald B. Trump. *Exploring Child Behavior.* Philadelphia: W. B. Saunders, 1976.

Wade, Carole. "What kids learn from rough and tumble play." *Working Mother,* February, 1989.

Weiss, Robert S. *Staying the Course: The Emotional and Social Lives of Men Who Do Well at Work.* New York: Free Press, 1990.

White, Burton L. *The First Three Years of Life.* New York: Avon Books, 1978.

Whiting, B. B., and C. P. Edwards. *Children of Different Worlds: The Formation of Social Behavior.* Cambridge, Mass.: Harvard University Press, 1988.

Winn, Marie. *Children Without Childhood.* New York: Penguin, 1983.

Yogman, M., et al. "Development of Infant social interaction with fathers." Paper presented at the meeting of the Eastern Psychological Association, New York, 1976.

Index

fathers exluded from close relationships with, 4
fearing loss of, 138
impact fathers can have on, 6
number of men interested in staying home with, 21
personalities and characters of, 37
resourcefulness of, 247
self-respect and confidence of, 108
sense of responsibility in, 108
socially competent, 92
undisciplined, 109
unpredictability of, 106
what fathers can learn from, 265–66
Clarke-Stewart, K. Alison, 45, 59
clay, 223–24
collecting, 231
computers, 231
concrete operations stage, 171
construction projects, 237
crayons and markers, 224–27
crying:
reasons for, 145–48
sleep problems and, 154–55, 157
tantrums and, 154

daughters:
authoritative fathers' influence on, 94
fathers' effect on intellectual development of, 97–98
permissiveness with, 86–87, 97
physical affection for, 187
sexuality of, 102–3, 178, 191–92, 197–98
dilemmas of fathers, 20–42
and competing demands of family and career, 8–13, 18, 20–22, 24, 28–31, 38, 60–62
components of, 23
and definitions of manhood, 27
and factors influencing involvement, 35–37
family negotiations for resolution of, 37–42
and increasing tension with children, 34–35
men's perspectives on, 28–31
mothers and, 9–12, 22, 24–28, 31–34
during pregnancy, 31
roots of, 22–24
in single- vs. dual-career families, 27–28
discipline:
by authoritarian fathers, 106, 109–10, 126–27
as complex issue, 104
confusion about control and, 105–7
difficulties with, 105
intermittent reinforcement schedules in, 114
as male responsibility, 105
potential harmfulness of, 109–10
power struggles as result of, 126–27